END
UNEMPLOYMENT
NOW

END
UNEMPLOYMENT
NOW

How to Eliminate Joblessness, Debt,
and Poverty Despite Congress

RAVI BATRA

palgrave
macmillan

First published in 2015 by PALGRAVE MACMILLAN® TRADE
in the United States—a division of St. Martin's Press LLC, 175 Fifth
Avenue, New York, NY 10010.

Palgrave® and Macmillan® are registered trademarks in the United
States, the United Kingdom, Europe and other countries.

ISBN: 978-1-137-28007-7

Library of Congress Cataloging-in-Publication Data

Batra, Raveendra N.
    End unemployment now : how to eliminate joblessness, debt, and
poverty despite Congress / Ravi Batra.
  pages   cm
    ISBN 978-1-137-28007-7 (hardback)
    1. Unemployment—United States. 2. Manpower policy—United
States. 3. Small business—United States. 4. Fiscal policy—United
States. I. Title.
HD5724.B3458   2015
331.13'770973–dc23

                                                  2014039420

Design by Letra Libre, Inc.

First edition: May 2015

10 9 8 7 6 5 4 3 2 1

Printed in the United States of America.

The goal of macroeconomics is
To raise the living standard of all
To erase poverty and unemployment
For people big and small

CONTENTS

ACKNOWLEDGMENTS

MY LATE TEACHER SHRI P. R. SARKAR, A MAN OF REMARKABLE INTELLECT and courage, once said to me, "Your goal in life should be to find a way to eradicate poverty around the world." It was 1964 and at the time I was a mere student at the Delhi School of Economics; I had no pretensions that I could ever accomplish such a task. Two points stood out in my teacher's theories. First, the foundation of prosperity is people's purchasing power; second, rising inequality eventually destroys any economy. I have written many books to demonstrate how excessive inequality of income and wealth generates recessions, depressions, and even revolutions, but this is the first one in which I have been able to offer practical methods for eliminating poverty around the globe.

According to Shri Sarkar, we live in the age of acquisitors, or what he called *Vaishya Rajyam*. I have been and will remain grateful to my teacher for pointing my thoughts in the right direction. Almost everyone can now see what extreme wealth concentration has done to the US economy.

I also offer my heartfelt gratitude to my editor, Karen Wolny, whose infectious enthusiasm enabled me to finish this work on time. Others who helped me with this project are my research assistant, Ani Harutyunyan, and my family, who edited all chapters. Thanks are also due to my friends Thor Thorgeirsson, Rajani Kanth, and

Satish Gupta for their encouragement as I undertook this writing. In addition, Clifford Thompson and Alan Bradshaw did a great job with the copyediting work. The Maguire Center for Ethics and Public Responsibility at SMU kindly provided support for my research. Finally, the work actually started in 2010, when I discussed some of my ideas with then House Speaker Nancy Pelosi, whose enthusiastic reaction to them prodded me to put in long hours of research and eventually come up with something that could really help me achieve my lifetime goal of eradicating global poverty.

PREFACE

THIS BOOK HAS BEEN IN THE MAKING FOR FIVE YEARS. IT AROSE OUT OF MY two-hour discussion with then House Speaker Nancy Pelosi, who visited Dallas in August 2010 in order to attend a fund-raising dinner for Texas Democrats. A prominent businessman and good friend of mine, Satish Gupta, called me the day she arrived and asked if I would like to have an audience with Ms. Pelosi at a hotel in downtown Dallas. I often talk to Satish about the state of the economy; he said, "I like your ideas, but let's see if they would fly with someone who is directly involved with our nation's politics. Are you prepared to see how Nancy reacts to them?"

I asked Satish, "Why would she want to talk to me? I have never met her before; nor have I made a contribution to anybody's election campaign." He said, "I am going to see her today and you can come with me as my guest."

I tagged along with Satish and his family, and we reached the hotel at noon. Apparently, he knew the House Speaker very well, because her secretaries greeted him warmly upon our arrival and asked us to sit around a table reserved for us. They addressed each other on a first-name basis, and we did not have to wait long before Ms. Pelosi came out of her suite. She stressed the need for electing more Democrats to Congress in order to fix the still-sputtering economy, in which jobs were very hard to come by. After chatting with Satish and his family for about 30 minutes, she turned to me and said, "You must be the Ravi Batra I have heard so much about."

I was startled, to say the least. Apparently, Satish had informed Ms. Pelosi's staff about his last-minute guest, and they indeed had looked me up on the Internet. I was pleased to see how thorough she was in her dealings. I said to her, "It's a shame that the Republicans obstruct the president at every step, even when he adopts their own proposals. But there is a way out of the quandary that has trapped our system. There are many things that he can do without recourse to Congress to quickly revive the economy and create millions of new jobs without raising debt."

At this point, I realized I had spoken too much without being asked. I had also mentioned something I shouldn't have, for federal debt was a touchy subject with the Democrats. However, Ms. Pelosi became very curious about my views and asked me to explain them further. After that our conversation went something like this:

I said, "There are many laws that authorize federal agencies to act on their own and generate competition in our markets. These agencies work for President Obama, who can persuade them to create free markets, and the Republicans should have no objection to something that makes the markets more competitive. It is because of the lack of competition that our consumers and workers have to pay high prices, earn low wages, pay high interest rates on credit cards, and so on."

Ms. Pelosi then asked me to elaborate my ideas further. I spent the next 60 minutes explaining to her the main cause of joblessness and growing poverty, as well as how the president on his own can bring credit card interest rates down to 5 percent, reduce the price of gas to about $1.50 a gallon, have the Federal Reserve do something to balance our foreign trade, etcetera. All this can be done while lowering our debt.

Ms. Pelosi was thrilled to hear my ideas. She wanted to have an extended discussion, but many others were waiting in the lobby for her. So she invited me to be her guest at the evening dinner, at which she was scheduled to address some of her supporters. In the meantime, she offered to get hold of Mr. Ben Bernanke and introduce me to him on the phone. Congressional elections were on their way in November, and she appeared eager to do something dramatic that could capture the nation's attention and, at the same time, rapidly end the ongoing specter of high unemployment.

At this point, Satish interjected, "Ravi, I have never heard you speak like this before. These ideas are new and I am sure they would work." Then, turning to Ms. Pelosi, he said, "Ravi and I are ready to fly to DC and give a presentation to anyone interested in learning the details."

Later that evening, Ms. Pelosi occasionally glanced at me and talked about the Democrats being a party of new ideas, and how such ideas would work their wonder for the middle class. At the end of the dinner, she told me that Mr. Bernanke was out of town but she would be in touch and invite me to DC soon.

That was the last time I spoke with her. Mr. Bernanke was perhaps not interested in my views about creating competition in various markets. As for Ms. Pelosi, she was no longer the Speaker following the 2010 elections. So here in this book, I build upon the ideas that caught her rapt attention. I am grateful to her for granting me an audience, and her positive reaction to my theories assures me that they were and are logical and can rid the nation of debt, joblessness, and poverty.

PART I

THE DIAGNOSIS

CHAPTER 1

INTRODUCTION

ON JANUARY 1, 2000, THE WORLD WAS DOUBLY EUPHORIC. THE CELEBRA-
tions were not only for a new year but also for a new millennium.
Nineteen ninety-nine had ended with the Dow Jones Index (Dow)
at 11,497, having risen from 2,634 at the end of 1990, or by an eye-
popping 336 percent in just a decade. Those invested heavily in share
markets rejoiced, and they expected more of the same in coming
years. Nothing on the horizon seemed to spell trouble, as the globe
was relatively at peace and prospering.

However, myopia seems to have clouded people's vision. The
new millennium opened with a host of unprecedented events and
problems. Polarization became the order of the day, and social divi-
sions surfaced in a way not seen in recent years. For the first time in
history the US Supreme Court intervened decisively in an election.
At the end of 2000, Mr. George W. Bush was declared, not elected,
president, even as his opponent, Mr. Albert Gore, won the popular
vote. The declaration was made after 36 days of relentless litigation
about who had won in the state of Florida, leading to great rancor

and mistrust among politicians and their supporters. Then came the 9/11 massacres in 2001, followed by the wars in Afghanistan and Iraq.

The Iraq conflict was especially divisive and led to great loss of life and money, while the nation was torn apart. Nothing like this had afflicted the United States since the Vietnam War. To top it all off, 2007 witnessed the start of a deep economic slump, whose effects were still being felt seven years later. In short, what a difference a decade made. The 1990s resembled the go-go decade of the 1920s, while the 2000s were reminiscent of the despairing 1960s.

Some experts call the 2000s the lost decade, one that seems to have continued into the 2010s. Not surprisingly, Americans now mistrust political leadership, as troubles pile up with no relief in sight. The president seems to be thwarted by Congress, a body that inspires especially little confidence. With the nation mired in poverty, joblessness, and a mountain of debt, both domestic and foreign, the public feels a deep-seated need for a fresh approach to our economic problems. And a fresh approach is exactly what this book offers.

First, I will demonstrate that the main cause of our myriad troubles is monopoly capitalism, a system dominated by giant companies; so the solution lies in returning to free markets and competitive capitalism, in which small firms engage in price and quality competition. But doing so would require new legislation and the cooperation of Congress, which itself is either divided or beholden to monopoly capitalists. While competitive capitalism seems to be a panacea for most of our ills, how do we bring it about, when the interests of the wealthy are completely at odds with it? Well, there is a way, a very simple and foolproof way, out of this quagmire.

It turns out that the president can bring about a competitive-capitalism *effect,* though not free markets, without recourse to Congress. I trust our president more than I trust the legislative bodies, and a competitive-capitalism effect is all we need to solve the problems of debt, poverty and joblessness. In order to generate free markets, we would have to break up the numerous conglomerates that dominate the nation's economy, which our Congress would never allow. Besides, we have lost precious time and money trying to fight the slump through conventional, debt-increasing approaches. We need to end poverty and unemployment now. And believe me, this can be done by any president of the United States within two years.

A competitive-capitalism effect occurs when, through certain simple proclamations or policies, a market arrives at the same outcome that would prevail in the presence of small firms operating as competitive enterprises. This already occurs in some cases. For instance, take the case of regulated enterprises that exist in most localities, offering water, electricity, and natural gas, among other necessities. These public utilities are called natural or regional monopolies. In other words, there is only one firm that supplies the needs of a large area. An example is the California Water Service Company, which is one of many firms that supply water in the state of California. The San Jose–based firm serves about half a million customers, and its rates are set by the California Public Utilities Commission (CPUC).[1]

Since water is a necessity, Cal Water could abuse its monopoly power and charge a high price to its local customers. The company, actually a conglomerate of several water supply firms, is a regional monopoly. There are two ways to prevent the firm from abusing its customers. Either break up the conglomerate and create competition among its subsidiaries, or have its rates regulated by an independent party such as the CPUC, so that its prices reflect free-market outcomes. Such regulation generates a competitive-capitalism effect, though not a free market itself. But the result is the same.

In a similar way, the president can create a competitive-capitalism effect in several industries without splitting giant firms that have corrupted our economy and politics since at least 1981. He can do this in the areas of banking, oil, health care, foreign trade, retailing, and housing, among many others. I will demonstrate all this in the chapters that follow, with the help of numerical examples, history, and simple logic.

It is an open secret that Congress's job-approval rating is near its all-time low. Capitol Hill has not been very cooperative in helping President Obama end joblessness and poverty. However, my point is that the president, and possibly the Federal Reserve, alone can end this scourge in a very short period. *Congress can be excluded from the highly desirable task of restoring prosperity to America.*

The book is divided into two parts. Part I illustrates the various causes of unemployment. Here I offer a new idea—namely, that the ultimate source of joblessness is monopoly capitalism, which enables industrial giants such as ExxonMobil and IBM, among countless others, to charge exorbitant prices while restraining wages and extracting huge productivity from employees. This creates overproduction, hence layoffs. Rising productivity augments the supply of goods and services, whereas high prices and low wages restrain consumer demand. In this way production and supply constantly exceed demand, so that either there are layoffs and wage stagnation or few entrants to the labor force are hired.

Part II offers ways in which the government can generate something similar to free markets without new legislation. This is the crux of my idea for creating jobs. We cannot count on Congress to break up the industrial behemoths and produce competitive capitalism, because these giants are the paymasters of elected officials. However, I will demonstrate that the president and the Federal Reserve themselves can generate free-market conditions that will quickly end the specter of unemployment.

The entire argument will be explained in the chapters that follow. Chapter 2 introduces the reader to the reasons why the legislature has become a do-nothing Congress; chapter 3 describes the full extent of the unemployment problem, whereas chapter 4 deals with the theory of free profit, which is the central idea underlying monopoly capitalism.

Chapter 5 explores various causes of unemployment. Here we find that the main reason for joblessness in an advanced economy is a rise in the gap between labor productivity and wages, a theory that I have previously explored in two books, *Greenspan's Fraud* and *The New Golden Age*.[2] This is because productivity is the main source of supply, while wages are the main source of demand, and the rise in the gap generates an excess of supply over demand, thereby creating overproduction and layoffs. Next I argue that this rise results chiefly from monopoly capitalism; therefore, in order to ensure that wages keep up with the ever-rising productivity, the government should either bring about free markets or create the competitive-capitalism effect through other means.

Chapter 6 explores the anatomy of bubbles that eventually burst and transform an ordinary slump into a mega-recession, even a depression. In chapter 7 we examine how monopoly capitalism generates a relentless rise in the wage gap as well as in the nation's debt. Chapter 8 narrates the story of a political debate among three candidates for a Senate seat.

From chapter 9 on we analyze ways in which joblessness can be quickly eliminated without requiring new legislation. This chapter explains how a free-market effect can be created in the areas of finance and banking, the credit card industry, and retailing. Chapter 10 shows how competitive effects can be generated in oil markets, whereas chapter 11 does the same in the arena of foreign trade and pharmaceuticals, demonstrating how a policy of balanced free trade alone would create at least five million jobs in manufacturing industries in just one year. In chapter 12 we look at the emerging market economies and at ways to generate jobs there without excessive dependence on the US and European markets. Chapter 13 sums up my entire argument, namely, that free markets, as preached by Adam Smith, offer the best ray of hope for escaping our vicious circle of grinding poverty, debt, and unemployment. Finally, chapter 14 offers a technical appendix to demonstrate the bankruptcy of macroeconomics prevalent today.

So now relax and read a simple economics book as if you are reading a novel.

CHAPTER 2

A DO-NOTHING CONGRESS

WHEN MR. BARACK OBAMA WAS FIRST ELECTED PRESIDENT OF THE UNITED States, Americans of all stripes—Republicans, Democrats, and Independents—looked forward to better days. The nation's economy was in a free fall, with thousands of workers laid off every month. Almost everyone—whites, blacks, Hispanics—had already suffered grievous pain. Mr. Obama's rise to the pinnacle of power itself was unprecedented, and, at the start of the election season, few experts had given him a chance. But Mr. Obama defied the odds. For the first time in history, a black person had become a presidential nominee; he then went on to defeat his Republican opponent, Mr. John McCain, in a landslide yet. Mr. Obama's victory was all the more astounding because Mr. McCain was a war hero and commanded great respect from his Senate colleagues.

Following the election, Americans felt that, with the Democrats also controlling the House and the Senate, a major change was in the offing. But the Senate, with its peculiar operating rules, such as the permitted use of the filibuster, was able to thwart virtually all of

Mr. Obama's ambitious plans, although in the process the legislative bodies earned the reputation of a "Do-Nothing Congress."

However, this was not the first time that lawmakers were in horrendous disrepute; it was President Harry Truman who had coined that phrase in 1948, irked by a Republican-controlled Congress that sought to undo some of the laws enacted under President Franklin Delano Roosevelt. Ever since then, the nickname has symbolized the inaction and ineptness of lawmakers. At mid-2014, however, the reputation of Congress was at its all-time low. How did all this come to pass?

On Election Night, November 4, 2008, the president-elect gave one of the best speeches of his meteoric career. He spoke with courage and candor:

> But above all, I will never forget who this victory truly belongs to. It belongs to you. It belongs to you. . . . This is your victory.
>
> And I know you didn't do this just to win an election. And I know you didn't do it for me.
>
> You did it because you understand the enormity of the task that lies ahead. For even as we celebrate tonight, we know the challenges that tomorrow will bring are the greatest of our lifetime . . . a planet in peril, the worst financial crisis in a century. . . . There's new energy to harness, new jobs to be created. . . .
>
> The road ahead will be long. Our climb will be steep. We may not get there in one year or even in one term. But, America, I have never been more hopeful than I am tonight that we will get there. I promise you, we as a people will get there.[1]

Mr. Obama gave hope to millions of people that night. Those who were jobless, were subsisting on unemployment benefits and food stamps, or had seen the value of their 401(k) retirement plans plummet in a major stock market crash wished him success from the bottom of their hearts. Alas, even in 2014, some six years later, President Obama had been proven right in only one of his predictions, namely, "We may not get there in one year or even in one term." Americans were no longer certain if better days would ever come again.

To be sure, the president succeeded in enacting a historic first— the Affordable Care Act—and by the end of his first term, in early 2013, the economy was no longer in a free fall. The stock market had recovered nicely, and a few million jobs had been created in four years. However, all this had come at an enormous cost. The nation was no longer desperate, but progress had been miserably slow. Federal debt had skyrocketed from less than $10 trillion on the eve of his election to over $16 trillion in 2012; fewer people were employed that year than in 2006; the poverty rate was the highest in 50 years, while the nation's foreign debt showed no signs of abating. The majority of Americans were ambivalent about their economic future.

It seems like a miracle that Mr. Obama was re-elected. The general election of 2012 was, to say the least, acrimonious. Both Democrats and Republicans blamed each other for the unending plight of the economy. In fact, that acrimony had started almost on the day Mr. Obama was sworn in, on January 20, 2009. The president had an ambitious agenda of change, whereas his opponents had an equal determination to thwart him. His first major move was to engineer a stimulus package that would offer immediate aid to the needy. Officially known as the American Recovery and Reinvestment Act (ARRA), it proposed to assist the unemployed and provide funds to some states that planned to cut essential services or raise local taxes.

The ARRA resembled what is generally known as the Bush bailout plan enacted the year before, but Republicans were now wary of adding to the sky-high budget deficit. While the measure passed despite their opposition, it sowed the seeds of mutual suspicion between the political parties.

Then came the president's State of the Union address to a joint session of Congress, in which Mr. Obama offered his vision of what he proposed to achieve over the next four years. He first spelled out a litany of what was wrong.

> The fact is, our economy did not fall into decline overnight. Nor did all of our problems begin when the housing market collapsed or the stock market sank. We have known for decades that our survival depends on finding new sources of energy. Yet we import more oil today than ever before. The cost of health care eats up more and more of our savings each year, yet we keep delaying reform. Our children will compete for jobs in a global economy that too many of our schools do not prepare them for. And though all these challenges went unsolved, we still managed to spend more money and pile up more debt, both as individuals and through our government, than ever before.

Then he offered his solutions for these problems:

> The budget I submit will invest in the three areas that are absolutely critical to our economic future: energy, health care, and education.[2]

Those words represented the defining moment of Mr. Obama's presidency, convincing Republicans that he was a socialist masquerading as a reformer. Mr. Obama, they thought, wished to extend governmental reach, which they vehemently opposed. Within weeks the president supported a budget that added hundreds of billions of dollars to the already bloated government spending, and Republicans declared it "dead on arrival." It grossly underestimated the true level of the deficit and reminded people of the same chicanery that had made Congress a laughingstock in the past.

The proposed budget contained myriad earmarks, or specific spending items that individual members of Congress insert into legislation. They are often called "pork," whose only purpose is to increase government spending in a given representative's own district. Most of them offer little social benefit, but virtually all lawmakers have sought them for decades.

During the election campaign candidate Obama had decried the earmarks, but in March 2009 he signed a law that contained thousands of them. Even some of his supporters were disappointed, because the legislation generated wasteful spending when the annual deficit already exceeded $1.4 trillion. Besides, it looked like business as usual, which the new president was not expected to tolerate.

Clearly, the president's dealing with Congress was off to a poor start. Initially, the disputes were ostensibly over ideology and policies, but soon they seemed to become personal. Republicans simply had little respect for their new commander in chief. On September 9 the president addressed Congress to tout his plan for universal health care. At one point during the speech, a Republican House member, looking directly at the president, shouted, "You lie."[3] Though the outburst was condemned by both parties, it underlined the disdain that some Republicans heaped on the president. Disagreement with someone is one thing; heckling the leader of your country during his speech is something else.

Health care legislation was a particularly sore point for the GOP. After the law was passed, in 2010, Republicans made countless attempts to undo it. Needless to say, its constitutionality was challenged, but the Supreme Court upheld most of its provisions in 2012 with a 5–4 majority.

There was seemingly no end to prickly issues. Even when the president adopted some provisions of the Republican agenda, such as trimming the payroll tax rate, the GOP lawmakers would oppose him at the time of legislation. Mitch McConnell, the Senate minority leader at the time, once remarked, "*The single most important thing we want to achieve is for President Obama to be a one-term president.*"[4]

THE TEA PARTY

Mr. McConnell's hopes surged after congressional elections in November 2010, when Republicans retook control of the House. Federal debt and deficits were major issues during the elections, and the GOP made the most of them.

Following their victory, Republicans felt vindicated in their quest to restrain the budget deficit that had been spiraling out of control. Democrats, including the president, were shocked by the loss of dozens of seats in the House—63 to be exact—and six in the Senate. Now the government was even more divided than before, with the House solidly controlled by the GOP, the Senate still under the Democratic hold, albeit with a smaller majority, and the presidency remaining the same. The political landscape had changed overnight. Although unemployment was still very high, many people, especially conservative experts, openly questioned the strategy of creating jobs through runaway government spending—and were suddenly able to act on their own beliefs.

Meanwhile, a new political force had emerged on the American horizon—the Tea Party, which is made up of splinter groups in different states whose common agenda is to trim the federal debt and budget deficit. The party favors drastic cuts in federal spending but opposes any rise in tax rates to reduce the deficit. It draws inspiration from the original Boston Tea Party episode in 1773 that sparked the American Revolution. The movement, which started in 2009, stood apart from other antitax protests by blaming both Republicans and Democrats for piling up the federal debt.

At first no one took the group seriously, because the various factions in the movement—a blend of conservative, libertarian and populist groups—did not seem to have much in common and so did not appear to present a threat; but then Mr. Scott Brown, a Republican candidate, won a special election in the Democratic stronghold of Massachusetts in January 2010, partly with active support from the Tea Party. The event captured national headlines, because a Republican had won the seat held by the late Senator Ted Kennedy, who had been an icon for Democrats for decades. This was a coup d'état in a blue state, and it could not but have widespread repercussions.

Soon the Tea Party became a household name; the zeal of its members especially impressed Republicans, who had been trying their best to wrest control of Congress. Finally, with the help of the Tea Party, the GOP succeeded in November 2010. This was a grim premonition of things to come, because several unprecedented and contentious events were to take place one after another.

First, there was the matter of raising the federal debt ceiling, which was set to expire in March of the next year. By law an administration can spend only the funds in its possession; the funds may come from tax revenue or from borrowing, the limits of which are set by Congress. In other words, the debt ceiling is like an upper limit on a credit card. The legislature periodically raises this limit so that the government can honor its spending commitments; otherwise, there is a danger of defaulting on the debt, or of the government's shutting down, at least partially, because it can't pay for services.

Early in 2011, Republicans, especially those beholden to the Tea Party for their election victories, offered to raise the debt ceiling in exchange for a major reduction in the budget deficit. The deficit can be lowered through spending cuts or a rise in tax rates, but the GOP leaders en masse were opposed to any tax hike, even if it meant only eliminating loopholes. By contrast, Democrats preferred a small cut in spending coupled with a large rise in tax receipts.

Tax rates versus government spending thus became the main bone of contention. Neither party would budge, while the government inched closer to running out of funds. With mega-debts and mega-deficits, the government could not afford to renege on its commitments; it had borrowed money from people and nations around the world, and there was a real chance of debt default along with a global financial crisis. Finally, there was a last-minute agreement at the end of July, with a deficit reduction amounting to $2.1 trillion over 10 years, coming chiefly from cuts in defense and domestic spending.

The world breathed a sigh of relief, but the deficit reduction was not enough to placate Standard & Poor's, a rating agency, which downgraded the quality of the US debt one notch. While nothing like this had happened before, its consequences were short-lived. However, the crisis had been only postponed, because the debt-ceiling brawl would recur in 2013.

THE GOVERNMENT SHUTDOWN

Following Mr. Obama's re-election in 2012, Republicans, especially the Tea Party, were in despair. Having failed to prevent the president from winning again, in 2013 they went after the Affordable Care Act—calling it Obamacare—which Mr. Obama regarded as his stellar accomplishment. Their tactics changed. Since the Supreme Court had upheld the constitutionality of the act, they now set out to delay the enforcement of the law by denying it any funding. In mid-September the House passed an appropriations bill with this provision and sent it to the Senate, which stripped the House version of its Obamacare measure and sent the revised bill back to the House.

Undaunted, the House reinstated the measure and returned it to the Senate. This repeated back-and-forth cost precious time, and at the end of September, the deadline for the passage of a budget to fund government operations, no agreement had been reached. The nation watched this drama in horror, because, as expected, it led to the shutdown of the government on October 1, 2013. About 800,000 administration employees were furloughed, and another million were given part-time assignments.

Few could fathom why defunding Obamacare was more important to Republicans than the functioning of the government, especially at a time when the economy could not afford to face any disruption. Poverty was already at the highest level in 50 years, and a vast swath of Americans, including government employees, lived from paycheck to paycheck. In any case, the Affordable Care Act was already financed by new taxes that could not be repealed. The attempt to dismantle it was a futile exercise in gamesmanship that the Tea Party imposed on most Republican lawmakers as well as the nation. In fact, Obamacare went into effect on the day the government curtailed its operations.

October and November were the months when Congress's approval rating first hit a new low: less than 10 percent. Figure 2.1 displays a swift and sharp plunge in the popularity of lawmakers since 2001, when a united Congress acted promptly against the perpetrators of the 9/11 massacres and saw its popularity soar. The government shutdown, however, was just the latest in a series of missteps that had sent Congress's rating downward since then. The president's popularity also suffered, but a majority of the people blamed the shutdown on the Tea Party.

The shutdown lasted 16 days and left a scar on the American psyche. No branch of government was to regain its popularity in 2014, when Congress's rating hit another low at 7 percent. The public became extremely cynical about the political class. The burning

FIGURE 2.1: PERCENTAGE OF PEOPLE APPROVING CONGRESS'S ACTIONS

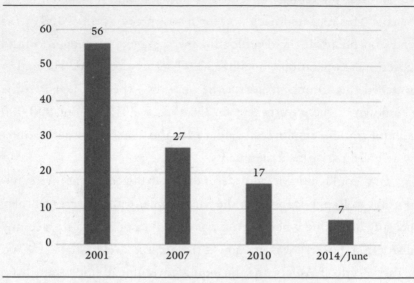

Source: Rebecca Riffkin, "Public Faith in Congress Falls Again, Hits Historic Low,"
Gallup.com, June 19, 2014.

question of the day was, and is, how this do-nothing Congress can
get anything done to relieve poverty and improve the living standard
of the poor and the middle class. In the pages that follow, I will
show you that the president himself can do many things to eliminate
unemployment and poverty very quickly, possibly by the end of his
term, without recourse to Congress. The legislative bodies can be
bypassed completely, because the agencies working for the president
already have all the authority they need to bring about at least a few
of the needed reforms.

CHAPTER 3

UNEMPLOYMENT

A Curse

WHEN SOMEONE LOSES A JOB, HE OR SHE SOON REALIZES THAT UNEMPLOY-
ment is painful; but when someone loses a job and can't find another
for months or years, that person knows firsthand that unemployment is a curse. Millions of people felt helpless and accursed in the
United States starting in 2007, when layoffs became common and
proliferated over the next two years.

Officially the unemployment rate peaked toward the end of
2010 at 10.8 percent, but if part-timers, discouraged workers, and
the under-employed are included, the figure reached as high as 17
percent of the workforce, or over 25 million people.

With an ailing economy, the Republican presidential candidate
had no chance of winning in the election of 2008. And, as pointed
out in chapter 2, the economy was so bad that Mr. Obama won
handily and took over the administration in 2009. The president
took office amid many expectations of his changing, possibly rev-
olutionizing, the political scene. Americans, especially production

FIGURE 3.1: NONFARM EMPLOYMENT BETWEEN 2006 AND 2014 (IN THOUSANDS)*

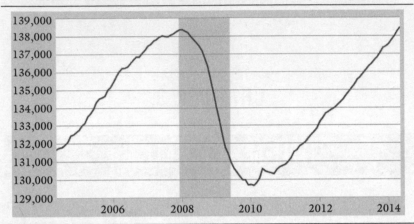

This graph is a reproduction from Federal Reserve Economic Data and has no title in the original. It shows that nonfarm employment in 2014 was essentially the same as in 2008.

Source: US Department of Labor, Bureau of Labor Statistics; Federal Reserve Economic Data, 2014.

workers, were very hopeful that the four-decade slide in their real wages would now be reversed through genuine economic reforms. But that has not happened. The new president did manage to enact a comprehensive health-reform bill that mainly helps the labor force, but in 2014, fully six years after his unprecedented victory, employment had barely caught up with its level in 2007. Figure 3.1 reveals that nonfarm employment peaked around 138 million in 2008 and did not regain that level until 2014, and only after the president added another $8 trillion to the federal debt.

Under the inspiration of old-guard economists, the president followed the same old policy of debt creation, but the debt growth now had to make up for the loss of consumer borrowing as well in order to raise the nation's demand artificially to the level of supply. He started off with another bailout—some $800 billion worth—like his predecessor. When that proved insufficient, he raised government spending further and cut payroll taxes. The end result was that federal debt rose from less than $6 trillion in 2001, when Mr. George W. Bush became president, to over $17 trillion in 2014. The debt had more than tripled in a matter of 13 years. This much is evident from figure 3.2, as federal debt soared from $5.6 trillion in 2000 to $17.8 trillion in 2014.

FIGURE 3.2: FEDERAL DEBT: 1980–2014

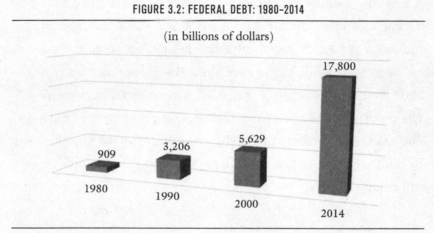

(in billions of dollars)

Source: *Council of Economic Advisers*, The Economic Report of the President, *2014*.

It wasn't always like this. Creating debt for the sake of prosperity is a relatively recent phenomenon. As demonstrated in the next chapter, numerically and historically, its main objective is to support the stock market and the excessive profits of bloated corporations in the name of preserving or generating jobs. *After all, in early 2014, under President Obama, corporate profits were close to their all-time high in an anemic economy.*[1]

The debt mountain of the new millennium should be examined in the context of what had occurred from 1789 to 1980, that is, from the birth of the American Republic to the end of Jimmy Carter's presidency. From George Washington to Mr. Carter there were 39 presidents, and at times their administrations borrowed money, mostly to finance major wars. Looking at the 1980 value in figure 3.2, it is clear that the total federal debt generated by all these presidents amounted to less than $1 trillion—over almost 200 years.[2] And then, in just six years under Mr. Obama, the debt had climbed by $8 trillion.

Evidently American prosperity was not built on the shaky foundation of red ink. Of course, corporate profits were not exuberant in the past, but jobs at decent wages were generally plentiful. Except during the calamity of the Great Depression, real wages and family income rose every decade. But in the new millennium, both wages and incomes have shriveled amid a rocketing federal debt.

Moreover, while employment in 2014 had caught up with the 2007 level, the poverty level had not, as can be seen from figure 3.3. The poverty rate jumped from 12.5 percent at the start of the recession to over 15 percent in 2012. In terms of the toll on families, over 10 million people joined the poverty rolls, and their numbers were still rising.

FIGURE 3.3: PEOPLE BELOW POVERTY LEVEL (IN %): 2007–2012*

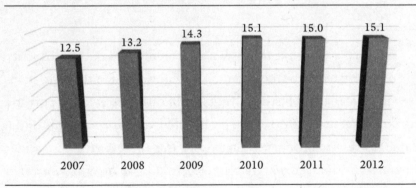

*"People below poverty level" is the standard measure of the rate of poverty.
Source: US Bureau of the Census, 2014.

GLOBAL REACH OF THE RECESSION

When America sneezes, so goes a cliché, the world catches a cold. But what happens if the United States catches a cold? Then I suppose the world catches pneumonia. This is what seemed to occur in 2008, when the American economy was in a free fall, and the rest of the globe began to shake and shiver. In retrospect, there were sad premonitions of hard times to come as early as July 2006, when home prices first began to decline. Normally this should not have mattered, because all industries have price fluctuations. But the United States, along with many other nations such as Britain, Spain, France, Australia, and Ireland, were trapped in housing bubbles at the time. Thanks to low interest rates and the reckless lending practices of large banks, average home prices had as much as doubled in these nations in just five years.

A lot of people had been buying real estate for speculation, expecting price appreciation for years to come. Some investors would purchase a house and then sell it six months later at a handsome profit. In this milieu the sudden decline in home prices in the United States came as a shock, because the value of securities tied to real estate plunged within days. A few months later, large banks and other financial institutions that had supported housing speculation with cheap credit were in a panic, facing the real prospect of insolvency. On August 9, 2007, central banks in several countries had to offer emergency loans to crumbling banks.

The housing market was not alone in terms of inflated prices. Bubbles had also formed globally in both the oil and stock markets. At first, these markets did not seem to notice any trouble in real estate, but after October 9, exactly two months following the central bank action, share prices sank precipitously. The Dow and the S&P index were cut in half over the next 18 months, along with similar declines all over the planet. Thus, what had started out as a minor price drop for American homes turned into a full-blooded financial crisis all over the world.

Naturally, with investor and consumer confidence in hurried retreat, output decline and layoffs followed soon, at first slowly and then with a crescendo. Almost six million people lost their jobs in the United States in 2008, and another 12 million in other countries. The world was frightened as the specter of a 1930s-style depression loomed large on the horizon. Some investors lost all their assets and, as during the Great Depression, committed suicide rather than face their irate lenders.

Joblessness in the eurozone stood at just 7 percent of the workforce in March 2008 but had climbed to an all-time high of 12 percent by February 2013. The highest rates occurred in Greece, Spain, and Ireland—over 20 percent. At least the unemployment rate in the United States fell, albeit slowly, following 2010, whereas in the euro area it barely budged.

FIGURE 3.4: UNEMPLOYMENT IN EURO AREA (IN %)

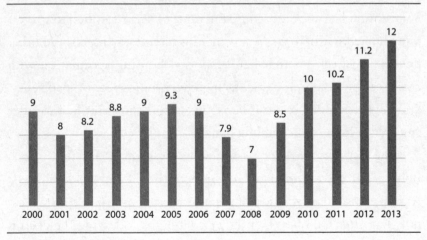

Source: Eurostat *2014.*

The Great Recession gave rise to a comical new acronym, PIIGS, which refers to five nations in the eurozone—Portugal, Italy, Ireland, Greece, and Spain. The slump hit these nations especially hard, so much so that their governments needed bailouts from the European

Central Bank (ECB). The US bailouts actually paled before those in Europe. The PIIGS suffered much higher interest rates for a while, and their unemployment rates far surpassed any experienced by other nations. The worst hit was Greece, with an unemployment rate over 27 percent even as late as 2013, something reminiscent of the Great Depression.

Other nations afflicted by the slump were India and China. They became part of another acronym, BRIC, a reference to Brazil, Russia, India, and China. However, the BRIC nations weathered the storm better than others. They did not suffer a drop in real gross domestic product (GDP), although unemployment went up somewhat. Their crises mostly occurred in the form of falling exports, especially for India, whose currency fell sharply relative to the dollar.

ECONOMISTS BLAME THE GOVERNMENT

With modern economies interlinked through the free flow of goods, services, capital, and technology, international trade and investment plunged quickly. The recession spread like a virus through this link-age. While the Great Depression was much worse than the recent slump, it did not spread its contagion so fast. Within a few months the Great Recession became global, and it continues to infect the world.

Most experts were caught off guard by the sudden turn of events, and now they blamed the disaster on the symptoms they observed. Some attributed it to the bursting of the housing bubble, while others found the culprit in the banking crisis. Still others heaped blame on official policies that encouraged deregulation, lax lending practices, and unprecedented consumer borrowing, but few held the real culprits, the wealthy oligarchs and monopoly capitalists, responsible.

See what the US Financial Crisis Inquiry Commission declared in its findings in January 2011:

The crisis was avoidable and was caused by: Widespread failures in financial regulation, including the Federal Reserve's failure to stem the tide of toxic mortgages; Dramatic breakdowns in corporate governance including too many financial firms acting recklessly and taking on too much risk; An explosive mix of excessive borrowing and risk by households and Wall Street that put the financial system on a collision course with crisis; Key policy makers ill prepared for the crisis, lacking a full understanding of the financial system they oversaw; and systemic breaches in accountability and ethics at all levels.[3]

Was the crisis avoidable? No. When the self-interest of the wealthy, not the welfare of the public, dictates government policy, how can any crisis be avoidable? Actually, the problems have occurred in the United States ever since 1981, when the tax system became ultra-regressive. Corporate and income tax rates fell sharply and eased the burden on the affluent, while all other taxes that hit the poor and the middle class soared. Thus, the Social Security tax, self-employment tax, gasoline tax, and some excise taxes all jumped in order to shrink the government budget deficit that resulted from the plunge in corporate and income levies.

When the tax burden is shifted from the affluent onto the backs of the destitute, the end result is a stagnant economy and eventually a horrifying recession or depression. This is because such a shift crimps consumer demand, which in turn discourages investment. A business, after all, can survive only if there is enough demand for its product.

Ever since the mid-1980s, I had argued that deep slumps and depressions result from excessive concentration of wealth, so that government policies should not encourage greed, business mergers, deregulation, and unchecked hoarding of wealth, all of which generate a variety of bubbles followed by crashes.[4] But the orthodox economists paid no heed. In their view the Great Depression had resulted from faulty government policies such as tariffs, high taxation, or insufficient printing of money, which indeed was partly true, but no one explained that the real drivers were and are the monopoly capitalists, whose wealth spoke loudly through hired experts. The oligarchs, not the ordinary people who elected the politicians and became the primary victims of the slump, decreed government policies. Thus the Depression was the handiwork of rulers acting behind the scenes, not of elected officials.

This time again the offending oligarchs, especially bankers at large financial institutions, have managed to hoodwink gullible economists. Some financiers even broke laws but have gone scot-free. When something like a bottomless downturn occurs, the causes are buried deep in the recent past, not in apparent symptoms. The seeds of the Great Depression were sown during the 1920s; the recession's seeds were sown during the 1990s and early 2000s. Let us not confuse the effect with the cause. All this will become clear in subsequent chapters.

CHAPTER 4

MONOPOLY CAPITALISM AND THE THEORY OF FREE PROFITS

TWO THOUSAND TEN WAS A CURIOUS YEAR. WHILE IT MARKED THE BEGINNING of a new decade of the new millennium, it was also the year when the National Bureau of Economic Research (NBER) declared the end of the Great Recession. The NBER is an independent body of economists that decides when a recession begins and when it ends, and most experts accept its proclamations. Its main criterion for dating a slump is the behavior of the gross domestic product (GDP), which is the sum total of goods and services produced in an economy. If output declines for two consecutive quarters, the NBER declares a recession, and then proclaims its end when GDP starts to rise. On this basis the Great Recession started in December 2007 and ended in June 2009, some 18 months later, which made it the longest downturn since the 1930s.

Although the GDP criterion worked well in the past, this time its invocation was dubious. The rise in output normally leads to a proportionate rise in employment, but not this time. The economy had shed more than six million jobs in 2008 and 2009, but few people had been recalled to work by 2010. Even President Obama, who should have celebrated NBER's claim, actually rejected it. "Obviously, for the millions of people who are still out of work, people who have seen their home values decline, people who are struggling to pay the bills day to day, [the recession is] still very real for them," he said.[1] In fact, a month after the NBER declared the end of the slump, civilian employment fell sharply, according to the *Economic Report of the President.*

Still, the NBER oracle is virtually regarded as gospel. Regardless of how the people feel, experts dare not oppose it. Thus, ever since 2010 almost every economist in the world has believed—or said— that the Great Recession lasted only 18 months. Some, especially the perennially optimistic Wall Street wizards, even assured us that prosperity was around the corner. Never mind that GDP growth averaged 2 percent between 2010 and 2014 and was clearly sub-par relative to the 5 percent mark that normally follows a recession. While growth was mediocre at best, corporate profits and the stock market broke record after record, especially in 2013, when the Dow jumped over 28 percent in one year.

The public surely disbelieved the NBER savants and Wall Street analysts. As late as May 2014, according to a Marist poll, 54 per-cent of those polled thought the nation was still in recession.[2] And why not? After all, even after seven years, civilian employment, at 144 million, was still below its level in 2007, when it exceeded 146 million.

In my previous book, *The New Golden Age,* written in 2006, I had predicted that a deep recession would start by the end of 2007 and last till 2016. It is clear that the public sides with my view, be-cause I believe that employment, wages, and poverty should be the major indicators of the state of any economy. It really taxes credulity to hear that the recession ended several years ago when fewer people are working now than when the slump started.

Even Janet Yellen, the first female Federal Reserve chair, appointed in early 2014, conceded that government policies had yet to make a significant dent in real wages and unemployment. The government and the Federal Reserve had spent trillions of dollars to fix the problem, but there was very little to show for all that spending. Why? What is the reason for this yawning failure of official ideology and economic policy? In two words: monopoly capitalism.

MONOPOLY CAPITALISM

Monopoly capitalism is a system wherein a few giant enterprises dominate many industries. It is not the same thing as a cabal of several monopoly firms, in which each producer supplies an entire market. In fact, a monopoly need not be a huge company; recall the case of public utilities, which meet the needs of water and electricity in their respective states. Such firms are regional monopolies that are tightly regulated by the government and so pose no threat to society.

However, giant firms are something else. They restrain output, charge higher prices, and control wages. In this way they offer fewer jobs and lower family income. Technically speaking, an industry consisting of a few conglomerates is known as an oligopoly. In most advanced economies today, oligopolies masquerade as agents of free enterprise. They hire an army of experts to push their agenda at universities, in newspapers, and through broadcast media and the legislative bodies. (Note that monopoly capitalism is also known by other names, such as crony capitalism, vulture capitalism, and so on.)

The CEOs of oligopolies may be called monopoly capitalists. They treat their companies as fiefs and pay puny wages to workers but reward themselves with high salaries, bonuses, stock options, and retirement plans. Regardless of whether the economy is healthy or anemic, their compensation keeps climbing.

A lot of experts have documented this phenomenon, but the study done by economists Lawrence Mishel and Natalie Sabadish is among the most comprehensive and clear-cut.[3] Some of their discoveries are astounding. For instance, on average a CEO earned some $807,000 in 1965 and $5.7 million in 1995, a jump of some 500 percent in real income. At least 1995 was a boom year in which the economy produced almost 600,000 jobs. CEO income peaked in 2000 but began to fall following the stock market crash that year. It had almost recovered by 2007, when another crash brought it tumbling down again. In 2009, however, it started to rise again while close to six million workers were laid off. By 2012 the average CEO income was over $14 million, and the employment recession showed no sign of ending. Figure 4.1 displays how dramatically CEO income has grown in the United States from 1965 to 2012.

FIGURE 4.1: CEO INCOMES IN THE UNITED STATES: 1965–2012

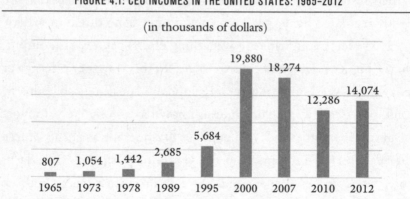

Source: Mishel and Sabadish, EPI.org, June 2013.

Another revealing item is the relationship of the CEO wage to the production wage earned by 80 percent of the labor force. In 1965 a CEO earned 20 times what a typical worker did; as shown in figure 4.2, this ratio climbed to 123 in 1995 and to an all-time high of 383 in 2000. After dropping for a few years, it had reached the level of

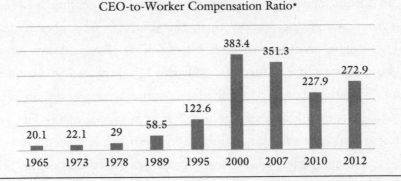

FIGURE 4.2: CEO WAGE RELATIVE TO THE PRODUCTION
WAGE IN THE UNITED STATES: 1965–2012

CEO-to-Worker Compensation Ratio*

1965	1973	1978	1989	1995	2000	2007	2010	2012
20.1	22.1	29	58.5	122.6	383.4	351.3	227.9	272.9

*CEO-to-worker compensation ratio is obtained by dividing annual CEO income by the wage of the production worker.

Source: Mishel and Sabadish, EPI.org, June 2013.

273 in 2012. No wonder the monopoly capitalist loves the system he controls.

A political system in which the wealthy control almost everything in society is known as an oligarchy, which is what we now have in the United States and much of the world. In other words, oligopoly breeds oligarchy. It is a system in which money determines virtually everything. Whether it is the economy, politics, elections, education, media, ideas, sports, even religion, the wealthy have a decisive say in it.

THE BIRTH OF OLIGARCHY

There was no oligarchy at the birth of the American Republic. US industrialization began with small companies that were unable to corner the market. But over time, because of business mergers, small firms turned into giants and began to restrain competition. Their monopoly power generated large profits that enabled them to offer bribes to politicians. This way they were able to get many laws enacted in their favor. During the 19th century some companies used child labor, while offering subsistence wages, and politicians did nothing about it. Businessmen's wheeling and dealing at the end of the 19th century earned them the sobriquet of robber barons. These men, according to economists Gilbert Fite and Jim Reese, "built poor railroads, turned shoddy products, cheated honest investors, sweated labor, and exploited the country's natural resources for their own wealth and satisfaction."[4] It appears Messieurs Fite and Reese could just as well be talking about modern businessmen.

Most industries had become oligopolies by the end of the 19th century, the beginning of the nation's sinking into an oligarchy. There was, of course, a populist reaction against oligopolistic exploitation. It eventually induced a reluctant Congress to pass an anti-monopoly law, known as the Sherman Antitrust Act of 1890, that barred collusion and the restraint of competition. The law did some good for society. For instance, it succeeded in breaking up Standard Oil, the largest conglomerate of all, into 16 smaller companies, including Exxon and Mobil. But after a few years most administrations became lax about its enforcement. Thus, monopoly capitalism survived and flourished again, especially after World War II.

FREE PROFITS OR FREE MARKETS

The ideological underpinning for crony capitalism comes from the view that free profits are superior to free markets. According to this theory, high profits are the main, perhaps only, source of economic prosperity, so nothing should be done to hinder the corporate pursuit of self-enrichment. Thus, there should be no enforcement of anti-trust laws; the minimum wage should be either kept constant or abolished; domestic competition among firms is not needed to ensure high efficiency and product quality, while foreign competition may be as high as possible; when big firms get into trouble, they should be subsidized; regulations should be kept on a leash; and so on. If firms transfer factories and jobs abroad to cut costs and maximize their income, say amen to them. The free-profit creed elevates business greed to a lofty pedestal. In its view, whatever enriches corporations—fraud, manipulation, bribery, collusion, conspiracy—enriches society.

Among the chief proponents of this view is a prominent economist and former Fed chairman, Alan Greenspan. Common sense suggests that there should be keen competition among companies to induce them to offer high-quality products at low prices. Otherwise they will pay no heed to customer complaints and charge as high a price for their goods as the consumer can bear. But Greenspan contradicts common sense by arguing that "it is precisely the greed of the businessman or, more appropriately, his profit seeking, which is the unexcelled protector of the consumer."[5] There are many other economists who hold the view that the freedom to maximize profits is more important than free markets in ensuring efficiency of production and a high standard of living.

Let us examine some history—past and recent. As Standard Oil was split among 16 companies in 1911, gasoline prices fell right away, while gasoline quality did not suffer. However, during the 1990s the government permitted the merger of many oil firms even though they were already minting money. Thus, Exxon and Mobil combined to form ExxonMobil, Chevron and Texaco became ChevronTexaco or CVX, and so on. Soon there were only five or six oil behemoths that dominated the market.

So what happened? See for yourself.

For starters, look at the international price of oil. From 1997 to 1999, just a few years ago, the rest of the world faced a minor recession, while the United States remained healthy. As global demand fell, the price of oil collapsed to $8.64 per barrel in December 1998. In the recent crisis the world economy was either stagnant or in recession for seven long years after 2007, and yet in mid-2014 the oil price hovered around $100 per barrel. US oil imports were well below their level in 1995, yet gasoline was far more expensive than before.[6] What has changed? The degree of competition! There are now only five or six companies along with OPEC that dominate the oil market, compared with just OPEC in the old millennium, and the cartel by itself was unable to prevent the oil-price collapse in a recession.

People constantly complain about exorbitant prices for medicines. Asthma is a chronic disease that afflicts nearly 40 million Americans but can be controlled with medicines. However, affording them is something else. A steroid inhaler such as Pulmicort may help, but it costs more than $175 in the United States, while in Britain the price is one-tenth as much for the same product. Another medicine, Aqua, retailed for $250 in California in 2013, while you could import it for just $7 from Europe.[7] Who is the culprit? Big Pharma, a code name for giant pharmaceutical companies such as Pfizer and Johnson & Johnson, among a few others. Under monopoly capitalism, everything seems to be big—Big Oil, Big Business, Big Banks, and so on. Few realize that the major causes of anemic job creation around the world are the shenanigans of these giant companies.

Why does monopoly capitalism continue to flourish when it has been disastrous for society time and again—when, as shown in the next chapter, it caused the Great Depression and now the Great Recession? The reason is simple. The wealthiest oligarchs are the rulers of America, and dethroning them can't be easy. But it can and will be done, because Americans will not tolerate an eroding living standard forever.

BAILOUTS AND CRISIS PROFITEERING

It is an old habit of monopoly capitalists, especially bankers and Wall Street oligarchs, first to generate a crisis and then to profit from it, a practice that might be called crisis profiteering. The primary goal of oligopolies is to make money by hook or by crook. During the great inflation of the 1970s, then Fed chairman Arthur Burns routinely printed money at the behest of Wall Street to fight the decade's several recessions. Not surprisingly, inflation surged out of control and climaxed into a severe slump. The oligarchs then discovered a friend in President Ronald Reagan, who blamed inflation not on excessive money printing but on budget deficits, which were tiny by today's standards. He curiously argued that deep cuts in income tax rates would actually slash the deficit by sharply raising GDP growth, which in turn would enhance tax receipts. Some called it "voodoo economics," but Wall Street offered it wide support. The top-bracket income tax rate plunged first from 70 percent to 50 percent in 1981 and then all the way to 28 percent by 1986. The wealthy took advantage of the inflation crisis by persuading politicians, both Democrats and Republicans, to trim their tax rates. The oligarchs smiled, but the vast majority of Americans chafed under a higher tax burden as payroll taxes soared.

Then came the savings-and-loan fiasco of the late 1980s. Many S&Ls went bankrupt between 1987 and 1989, and the government rescued them with a $250 billion bailout. Some of these financial institutions became solvent, only to be gobbled up by the oligarchs at dirt-cheap prices. The bankers profited handsomely from the crisis—once again.

In 2008 the United States faced a terrible credit crisis, and the bankers did the same thing all over again. They had engineered another catastrophe but benefited from it through yet another bailout. The bankers had made reckless loans and earned big profits, which turned into mega-losses when some of their borrowers defaulted. However, their friends in high circles came to their rescue, an arrangement contrived by a prominent financier, Hank Paulson, the treasury secretary under President George W. Bush and the former

CEO of Goldman Sachs. The $700 billion rescue plan, widely known as TARP (Troubled Asset Relief Program), was until then the biggest handout of all time. The bankers came out laughing, but the tax-payer had to foot the bill—once again. The plan did not even solve the economic problem, which stemmed from the excessive deregu-lation that was once championed by Goldman Sachs and Paulson himself. So now he perhaps felt guilty and came to the rescue of his buddies. If this is not oligarchy, what is?

President Bush signed the TARP law on October 3, 2008. Four days prior to the signing ceremony, I wrote an article about the pro-posed bailout, predicting that the law would do no good and could actually raise the price of oil back toward its prerecession level.[8] This is exactly what happened, and so the question is: What is the connec-tion between TARP and the price of oil?

First, let us briefly examine the oil-price trends in the new mil-lennium. As mentioned above, the petroleum price hit a low of $8.64 per barrel in 1998, when the world was in a minor recession from the so-called Asian Crisis. The price then slowly recovered, and in 2000 it averaged $27 per barrel. That is where it stayed, with routine fluc-tuations, until 2003, when for some reason it began a steady climb. Global demand and supply for oil were still in balance, so there was no earthly reason for the price to break away from its average. I suspected that some big companies were speculating in oil in a big way, and since Goldman Sachs was, and perhaps still is, among the ringleaders of speculators, I began to examine its oracles about oil. I observed an interesting pattern. The price of oil would usually rise soon after Goldman's research department predicted its rise.

I concluded that the company was engaged in creating the phe-nomenon of self-fulfilling prophecies, and minting money in the process. In 2007, the year the Great Recession started, oil averaged around $100 per barrel, rising to an all-time high of $147 in July

2008. By then the recession was in full swing, and no amount of speculation could keep the price from falling.

As TARP went into effect in October 2008, Goldman, a very profitable firm for many years, turned out to be a big beneficiary. I felt the TARP money would eventually raise the bonuses of most speculators, not just at Goldman but also at other Wall Street firms, so that oil speculation would return even at the whiff of economic recovery. The price plummeted to $31 in February 2009, as the economy continued to falter.

GDP stabilized in the second quarter of 2009, and not surprisingly, with speculators again pocketing hefty bonuses, oil speculation returned, at first slowly and then with gusto. The upward march of GDP was excruciatingly slow, but not that of oil, because by year's end the petrol price averaged around $68 per barrel. My worst fears were realized, as the price soared by $37 in less than a year: the oil barons were at it again. TARP was now hurting economic recovery, because the increasing price of oil and gasoline is like a hefty tax on the poor and the middle class. By the middle of 2014, oil hovered again around $100 per barrel, which is where it was just prior to the recession.

Thus, whenever a crisis appears, Wall Street jumps to the front row to profit from it. This is how monopoly capitalism has been slowly destroying America's middle class, with no one to stop it.

CHAPTER 5

WHAT REALLY CAUSES UNEMPLOYMENT?

A SAD HEADLINE CAUGHT MY ATTENTION IN 2013: ACCORDING TO THE CENSUS report, American poverty was the worst it had been in the last 50 years. I wondered why this was so, when corporate profits and share markets were booming and the government had been doing its level best since the start of the recession to erase destitution. Both the administration and the Federal Reserve had spent trillions to treat the malady, but with little success.

As 2014 opened, poverty headlines only became grimmer, as the old 50-year record was broken.[1] This is what happens when joblessness persists regardless of whether the recession is declared over. In order to end poverty, we need to end unemployment, and that takes us to the question of what causes it. That also opens the subject of why a recession occurs to begin with.

Most of you perhaps think that firms alone create jobs, but that is only partially true. In reality, job creation occurs through the cooperative action of both companies and consumers. Firms only provide the means to build products and, indeed, hire workers, but if their goods remain unsold, they lose money and workers are laid off. Both labor and capital are needed to start a business. Furthermore, the bulk of the demand for goods and services comes from workers. Thus firms supply goods and workers purchase most of them.

I am sure you've all heard of supply and demand, even if you never took a formal course in economics. Supply and demand are like the two wings of an airplane; they have to be equally strong and weighty, or else the plane will crash. In the same way, supply and demand have to be in balance to preserve jobs.

What is the main source of supply? Productivity. What is the main source of demand? Wages. If you become more efficient—through education or the use of better technology—you produce or supply more goods. If your wages go up, then you consume or demand more goods. For the economy to stay healthy and be free from job losses, supply must be equal to demand, or:

Supply = Demand

This is a simple equation, and please don't be alarmed by its use, because it will highlight the factors that underlie job creation. If supply and demand are not equal, then, like the airplane with uneven wings, the economy will crash someday. Here, supply refers to the value of goods produced in the economy, and demand means spending by consumers and investors on goods produced in the nation.

It so happens that, because of investment and new technology, productivity and thus supply grow year after year. This means that wages—hence demand—must also increase every year, and in the same proportion. Otherwise, the resulting imbalance creates unexpected problems. If real wages trail productivity growth, supply exceeds demand, leading to overproduction. Businesses are unable to sell all they can produce in their factories, and layoffs follow. Therefore, the only cause of unemployment in an advanced economy is the rise in the gap between what you produce and what your employer pays you. In a developing economy, joblessness results from insufficient supply; there simply are not enough manufacturing plants to provide work to job seekers. In an advanced economy, however, there are plenty of factories, but some of them stand idle because of deficient demand resulting from stagnant wages.

Now the question is who is at fault when unemployment occurs in the economy. There are some luminaries who, believe it or not, think that all unemployment is voluntary. In the past they were called classical economists; today they are known as neoclassical economists. In their view, unemployment is technically voluntary because workers either turn down job opportunities or simply stop their job searches altogether.[2] Not only is this absurd; it is patently illogical and false. Joblessness occurs only if your boss doesn't pay you enough to match your productivity resulting from hard work, education, and skills, because then national demand falls short of national supply. When the total output of workers like you exceeds total spending in the economy because of low wages, then there must be overproduction, and hence layoffs.

If you are diligent and honest and still get fired, then it is the employer's fault, not yours. If you are doing your job of being productive on the one hand and creating demand out of your salary on the other, then there is no reason for you to be laid off. If your spending falls or does not rise enough, then it is because your boss has not given you a raise or has cut your wages. At the macro level, insufficient spending means only that workers like you have produced so much for their companies that supply exceeds demand, so that some people have to be laid off because of excess production. Where, then, is the workers' fault in this entire process? It is the greed of employers, nothing else, that generates joblessness.

Neoclassical economists blame unemployment on workers, who in their view quit jobs when their wages fall, or who choose to be idle rather than work in unpleasant conditions. Neoclassical experts have championed this idea for more than 200 years. Never mind the Great Depression, which saw as much as 25 percent of the labor force starve, or nearly starve, or the Great Recession, during which, at one point, as many as 20 million American workers and their families faced hunger because of unemployment. The question is whether these people chose to be jobless or were forced into joblessness. I have argued that it is the greed of the employer, and nothing else, that generates large-scale unemployment. This theory derives simply from the concepts of supply and demand, and even a layman can comprehend that overproduction must lead to layoffs.

Joblessness creates problems not only for the unemployed but also for elected officials, because the unemployed still have the right to vote. Politicians seek to be re-elected by a happy electorate. They don't like unemployment any more than you or I do, which means they have to find creative ways to raise national spending, or demand, to the level of supply. They face two choices: either follow policies to raise real wages until they are proportionate to the level of worker productivity—which is only fair and ethical—or adopt measures to lure people into larger debt, so that consumers spend more, not through pay raises, but from increased borrowing. This way, official policies raise demand to the level of supply by generating artificial spending.

Luring the public into debt in order to get re-elected, I believe, is crass corruption. This corruption occurs because the politician, ever in need of campaign donations, doesn't like to offend business interests that love low wages. With wages trailing productivity since 1981, some experts appointed by elected officials have been following what is known as monetary policy, which tempts people into larger debt. This eliminates unemployment as spending rises to the level of supply, because now,

Supply = Demand + Consumer Borrowing

With monetary policy, the Federal Reserve prints more money to bring down the rate of interest, which in turn induces people to increase their borrowing, generating new debt. The interest rate is the price of money, and when the supply of something rises, its price falls. Thus when the Federal Reserve increases money supply, the cost of credit declines. However, the wage-productivity gap has been rising so fast that the government also had to raise its own spending and debt constantly, so that total spending matched rising supply of goods. (To avoid confusion, please note that in general the term "supply" refers to the supply of goods.) In this case:

Supply = Demand + Consumer Borrowing + Government
    Budget Deficit

Raising government debt to postpone the problem of unemployment is called expansionary fiscal policy. Now you see why our nation is awash in debt, at both the consumer and the government levels. Presidents and lawmakers have frequently used debt-creation policies to get re-elected, while giving the impression that they are doing American workers a favor by preserving their jobs. In reality, they are preserving their own jobs and, in the process, further enriching the rich, as will become clear from subsequent analysis.

By now I have given you a simple idea of why jobs are lost. Let us now look at some numerical examples to further illustrate the points made above.

THE WAGE GAP

There are two popular theories of unemployment—classical and Keynesian. They both seem to be inadequate, or else their proponents would have ended joblessness a long time ago. The classical theory says job losses occur if the real wage is too high, so that if wage rates fall, the problem will go away. Keynesian economics, by contrast, blames the problem on demand that is deficient relative to supply, which makes sense, but John Maynard Keynes, the founder of this school of thought, didn't tell us what keeps demand low for long. I will discuss the technicalities of both views in an appendix to this chapter at the end of the book. For now, I will use pure common sense to illustrate my theory of unemployment.

At the outset, let us suppose General Motors builds 20 cars and puts them up for sale. If only 15 are sold, then GM is stuck with five unsold autos, and then it has to lay off workers. In other words, if a business is unable to sell all it has produced, it has to fire some workers and produce only up to the level of demand for its product. Now let us extend this idea to the macro economy. As suggested above, if supply exceeds demand, layoffs follow.

Macro supply means the value of goods and services produced by the nation as a whole, and macro demand signifies the level of spending by consumers and investors on those products. Both of these factors are measured in dollars. For the time being, let us ignore the role of the government in generating demand through spending and taxation. For ease of understanding, let me repeat that economic balance occurs when

Supply = Demand

Supply is simply GDP, that is, the value of a nation's output in a year, whereas demand has two components. One is money spent by consumers out of their incomes, and the other is investment, which is money spent by firms and people on what are known as investment goods, such as capital equipment and newly built residences. Thus,

Demand = Consumer Spending + Investment

For now, assume that there is no borrowing of any kind. Let us suppose that supply at current prices equals $1,000, consumer demand (or spending) is $800, and investment equals $200. Then

Demand = $800 + $200 = $1,000 = Supply

Here we have an economy in balance, one in which supply equals demand, so that there are no layoffs. Let the wage rate fall in accordance with the prescription of the classical theory. Then consumer spending will fall, because your salary is the major determinant of your spending. Suppose this spending declines by $200. So now

Demand = $600 + $200 = $800 < Supply = $1,000

Since supply exceeds demand, there will be layoffs; so you see the classical theory is totally bogus. Instead of solving the problem, this approach makes it worse. In fact, investment will also fall because of a decrease in consumer spending, and more layoffs will follow. What about the Keynesian view? This one is indeed valid, but it does not tell us why demand may remain deficient for a long time, as it did during the Great Depression—and has since 2007.

Let us now define the concept of the wage-productivity gap, or, simply, the wage gap:

$$\text{Wage Gap} = \frac{\text{Labor Productivity}}{\text{Real Wage}}$$

in which the real wage is the purchasing power of your salary, and productivity is output per employee, or what you produce for a business. If productivity rises faster than the real wage, the wage gap grows. We have explored the classical case, in which the real wage falls and increases this gap. Now let us examine the other case, where only productivity increases, say, by 10 percent; supply, then, at current prices, also increases by 10 percent. Thus, supply is now $1,100. If the wage rate is constant, consumer spending and demand stay constant as well. Recall that initially the economy was in balance, with demand equaling $1,000. After the rise in productivity,

Supply = $1,100 > Demand = $1,000

Here again there will be layoffs because of overproduction. The real cause of joblessness must now be clear. *Whenever the wage gap rises, layoffs become inevitable. This is because productivity is the main source of supply and wages are the main source of demand, and if wages trail productivity, demand trails supply, and some workers become redundant.*

This theory does not depend on what happens to prices, which will fall somewhat as output grows and the rise in the value of goods produced is less than 10 percent. So some may argue that price declines would raise demand to the level of supply. However, with wages stagnant, supply would still exceed demand, culminating in layoffs. If prices were to plunge substantially, then there would be large-scale unemployment, as happened during the Great Depression, because sinking prices simply decimate profits and cause widespread job losses. (In any case, prices rarely fall nowadays, and their effect may be ignored.)

The idea developed above explains why demand may be deficient relative to supply for a long time. If productivity keeps rising and wages remain stagnant for long, as has been the case since 2007, then supply remains ahead of demand, so that there are either persistent layoffs or few entrants to the labor force are hired. And until the wage gap closes, that is, returns to the pre-recession level, joblessness or poverty will not go away. (What causes the wage gap to rise is discussed in chapter 7.)

BUDGET DEFICITS

The wage-gap theory presented above can explain many phenomena observed in the economy since 1980. As described above, the rising wage gap also gives rise to perpetual budget deficits, especially in a democracy where elected officials face voters every two, four, or six years. No politician likes to confront the electorate in a milieu of growing unemployment. So when the wage gap rises and layoffs begin, the politicians, as explained before, have a painful choice. They either must follow a policy that raises the wage rate and closes the wage gap, or face irate voters and lose their cushy jobs and positions of power.

In fact, we can calculate how much of a budget deficit is required to avoid layoffs. If Supply = $1,100 and Demand = $1,000, then there are unsold goods worth $100. If there is no consumer borrowing, then the budget deficit must equal the value of unsold goods, or $100, to close the supply-demand gap. On the other hand, if the budget deficit cannot rise to this level, then consumer borrowing is also needed to preserve economic balance. So in order to avoid job losses,

Value of Unsold Goods = Budget Deficit + Consumer Borrowing

Thus, now our theory must be restated: *Whenever the wage gap rises, either layoffs occur or debt must rise at the consumer and/or government level to preserve jobs.* If productivity keeps rising and wages remain stagnant for many years, then consumer and government debt will have to grow year after year to preserve jobs. This is what happened after 1980, as government policies stimulated productivity on the one hand and led to sluggish wages on the other.

CONCENTRATION OF WEALTH

The next puzzle to be solved is that of the soaring disparity of income and wealth observed in the United States since 1981. I will now demonstrate how official debt-creating measures known as monetary and fiscal policies make the rich richer, while offering crumbs to those who are laid off. There are two possible scenarios, one in which the government perceives a threat of layoffs, and one in which some people have been already fired. The budget deficit has persisted almost relentlessly ever since 1980, frequently even without unemployment. There was only one year, 1999, when there was a slight surplus. Deficits existed even in the 1960s and the 1970s, but because of their paltry levels, they may be ignored.

In the absence of joblessness, the deficit simply raises profits without benefiting the workers. When productivity and output rise by 10 percent, business revenue increases proportionately, and if wages—and therefore consumer demand—are stagnant, there is a potential for layoffs, which are averted by the deficit. In this way, employment and people's incomes stay the same. All that happens is a rise in business revenue of 10 percent, which raises profits. Thus, in the absence of unemployment, the fruit of the budget deficit accrues entirely to companies, with no benefit to workers.

The other case sees the government raise its deficit to combat increasing joblessness. If some are called back to work, usually at lower wages, then workers get some benefit from official policy, but in this case profits rise even further because of lower wage cost to employers. *Here, the fruit of the budget deficit goes mostly to producers.* In fact, I will demonstrate in the appendix that under some fairly realistic conditions, every dollar of the budget deficit and consumer borrowing goes into the pockets of the super-wealthy monopoly capitalists, whose earnings include salaries, bonuses, stock options, pensions, and realized capital gains. Thus, the government that the oligarchs control duly serves its masters.

History clearly supports my view that high budget deficits generate enormous incomes for the wealthy, and the relevant information comes from both the conservative and the liberal media. An article from the *New York Times*, a liberal newspaper, reveals that after-tax profits as a share of GDP were close to the highest in history under President Obama, at 9.3 percent, followed by his predecessor, President Bush, at 7.2 percent. They both amassed enormous federal debt, with President Obama in the lead. Thus high government debt generated huge profits, even though GDP growth in the new millennium has been low to mediocre.

An article from Marketwatch.com, a sister company of a conservative newspaper, the *Wall Street Journal,* tends to reinforce this view. The title says it all: "U.S. Corporate Profits Soar in 2012. Workers Get Little of It."[3] The article contains a graph showing that the profit share in 2012 was the highest since 1943. That is an interesting year for comparison, because 1943 was also the year when the federal debt ratio with respect to GDP was close to the highest in the 20th century, if not in history. The world was then caught in a do-or-die struggle with Hitler, and the US government had no choice but to have huge budget deficits to finance its war spending.

Figure 5.1 presents data only from 1976 to 2012 but clearly indicates that under President Obama profits were at the highest level since World War II. The liberal and the conservative media rarely agree on anything, but they both suggest that corporate profitability broke a record in 2012. In view of my analysis, it is not a coincidence that federal debt was extraordinarily high in both 1943 and 2012.

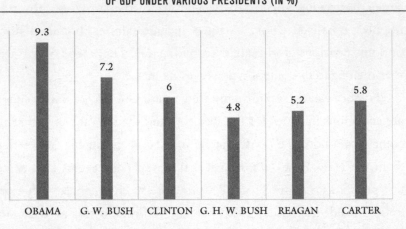

FIGURE 5.1: AFTER-TAX CORPORATE PROFITS AS SHARE
OF GDP UNDER VARIOUS PRESIDENTS (IN %)

Source: The New York Times, *April 4, 2014.*

Further confirmation of how high debt and high profits coexist comes from table 5.1 and figure 5.2. The table presents data for
the rate of profit from 1947 to 2011. The profit rate, which is what
a company earns as a percentage of its equity capital, yields a better picture of the affluence of firms than profit share. At 16 percent
this rate was extremely high in 1947, soon after World War II, but
it pales before the rate in the second quarter of 2011, which was 19
percent.

Now let's examine figure 5.2, which is a combination of two
graphs—a curved line depicting the debt and a series of bars display-
ing the rate of profit. The figure reveals that the debt-GDP ratio,
which exceeded 100 percent in 1947, fell steadily as the war debt
was retired over the years. It reached a low point around 1980 and
has risen steadily since. The rate of profit generally declined with the
debt ratio and began to climb as the ratio began to rise after 1980.
The graph reinforces the view that corporate profits benefit from
government deficits, which, in other words, tend to make the rich

TABLE 5.1: RATE OF PROFIT IN SELECTED YEARS (IN %): 1947–2011

1947	16
1950	15
1955	12
1960	9
1965	13
1970	9
1975	12
1980	14
1985	10
1990	11
1995	16
2000	15
2005	17
2011	17
2011 (Q2)	19

Source: Council of Economic Advisers, The Economic Report of the President, *1975 and 2013.*

FIGURE 5.2: FEDERAL DEBT AS SHARE OF GDP AND RATE OF PROFIT (IN %)

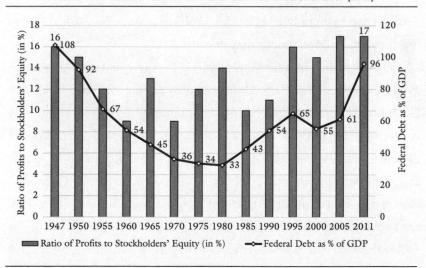

Source: Council of Economic Advisers, The Economic Report of the President, *1975 and 2013.*

richer. This, as demonstrated above by my theory, happened with or without unemployment.

In 1947 there was little joblessness, but the debt ratio was at its all-time high, and the profit rate was enormous. In 2011, when unemployment was widespread, debt was huge but below the previous high; yet the profit rate was higher. This is because joblessness had depressed wages relative to productivity. My analysis thus explains the paradox of the growing affluence of the oligarchs in a stagnant economy. See what a *New York Times* article says about the earnings of the super-rich:

> Hedge fund managers heavily populate the so-called 1 percent in the United States. And they are getting richer.
>
> The 25 highest-earning hedge fund managers in the United States took home a total of $21.15 billion in compensation in 2013.[4]

And the top earner made a cool $3.5 billion in one year. Who is helping them? The government they control.

The headline of the Marketwatch article mentioned above is even more revealing: "U.S. Corporate Profits Soar in 2012. Workers Get Little of It." Yes, indeed. As demonstrated by my analysis, this is precisely the outcome that a soaring wage gap along with a budget deficit generates. It is also confirmed by figures 5.3 and 5.4, which are reproduced from the 2014 *Economic Report of the President*. Figure 5.3 shows that the share of national income gobbled up by the top 1 percent of American families in 2012 matched the one in 1929, the year the Great Depression began. By contrast, figure 5.4 reveals how hard the Great Recession has been for American families generally. While the slump was supposedly over in 2009, real family income continued to decline, so much so that its level in 2012 fell short of that in 2000.

FIGURE 5.3: NATIONAL INCOME SHARE ACCRUING TO TOP
1 PERCENT OF FAMILIES: 1915–2012*

*This graph draws on the work of Thomas Piketty and Emmanual Saez.

Source: Council of Economic Advisers, The Economic Report of the President, 2014,
p. 41.

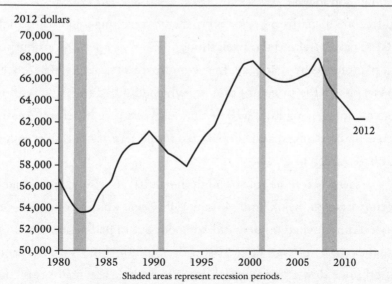

FIGURE 5.4: REAL INCOME FOR THE MEDIAN FAMILY: 1980–2012

Shaded areas represent recession periods.

Source: Council of Economic Advisers, The Economic Report of the President, 2014,
p. 36.

OTHER CAUSES OF UNEMPLOYMENT

While the main reason for joblessness is a relentless rise in the wage gap, there is one other cause that stands on its own, namely, a sharp increase in the price of oil, which affects both supply and demand. During the 1970s, OPEC, the international oil cartel, reduced its output and raised its price manifold, as much as 1,000 percent.

The United States was the largest oil importer at the time, and the nation's economy was hit very hard. Moreover, its oil use was very inefficient. General Motors and Ford Motor Company, among others, built gas-guzzling cars whose mileage varied between 10 and 15 miles per gallon. Airplanes were also gas-guzzlers. So the rocketing price of oil hurt both producers and consumers. Auto demand plunged while auto prices soared; similarly, airlines suffered huge losses. For the first time in its history the nation faced stagflation, a combination of rising prices and unemployment. A sharp increase in the price of oil, then, brings the worst of both worlds—high inflation and high job losses.

In 2008 also, the oil price skyrocketed, reaching an all-time high of $147 per barrel in July. Even though US oil use per unit of output had plummeted by that year, the economy reacted badly. There was a nasty rise in the price of gasoline, which climbed to $5 per gallon in some states, compared to half that level just a year before. Again, auto demand plunged and contributed to the severity of the recession that had started in 2007.

In recent years, the role of oil in the global economy has changed for the worse. In the old millennium, OPEC was able to control prices in good times, when oil demand zoomed, but in bad times, when oil demand fell, it suffered huge losses. Even minor slumps would bring the oil price down to as low as $10 per barrel. For instance, from 1997 to 1999, just 10 years prior to the Great Recession, the rest of the world faced a slight downturn, while the United States remained

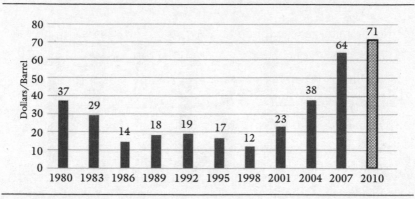

FIGURE 5.5: AVERAGE OIL PRICE IN THE UNITED STATES: 1980–2010

Source: Tim McMahon, "Historical Crude Oil Prices (Table)," InflationData.com.

healthy. As global demand for oil fell, the price dipped below $10 per barrel in some months in 1998, although for the year it averaged $12. Figure 5.5 illustrates the movement of petrol prices from 1980 to 2008, showing that they plunged to $14 per barrel in 1986 and went even lower 12 years later. Thus high oil would generally bring about a recession and low oil would contribute to ending the slump.

But not anymore. This time the world economy has been either stagnant or in recession since 2007, for seven long years, and yet the oil price hovered around $100 per barrel in May 2014. As mentioned in chapter 4, in 2014 US oil imports were below their 1995 level due to faltering oil demand, yet gasoline was far more expensive than before. Figure 5.6 makes this point vividly and shows that, on average, crude prices were the same in 2008 as in 2013, yet six million Americans were laid off in 2008, when oil demand plummeted because of a plunge in economic activity.

What has changed? The degree of competition! There are now two oil cartels, one belonging mostly to Middle East nations, and the other to the West. Only six companies, ExxonMobil, ChevronTexaco,

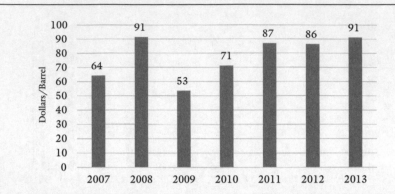

FIGURE 5.6: AVERAGE OIL PRICE IN THE UNITED STATES: 2007–2013

Source: Tim McMahon, "Historical Crude Oil Prices (Table)," InflationData.com.

BP, Royal Dutch Shell, Conoco Phillips, and Total SA, along with OPEC, dominate the global oil market, whereas OPEC alone did so in the old millennium, when the cartel by itself was unable to prevent the price collapse in shallow recessions. Three of these six are located in the United States, two in Britain, and one in France. Thus the monopoly power of two oil cartels dwarfs that of just one, and the world has to pay the price for its ineptness and inaction.

HIGH INTEREST RATES

Recessions and unemployment can also occur because of higher interest rates, which have a negative impact on consumer demand and business investment. Most people buy expensive goods such as autos, furniture, and appliances on credit, and high interest rates make them even more expensive, so consumer demand falls. Investment also drops. New residences as well as capital goods such as machines are considered investment goods. Consumer investment equals money spent on the purchase of new homes and apartments, whereas business investment is money spent by firms on new capital goods. Since the vast majority of families buy residences on credit, high interest rates discourage this type of spending. While business investment depends mostly on consumer spending on domestically produced goods and product prices, rising interest rates impact that spending negatively to an extent. Thus, if borrowing costs rise, consumer demand and investment decline relative to the supply of goods, resulting in overproduction and layoffs.

Normally, there is an extraneous reason for the spike in the cost of credit. High inflation generates high interest rates, which in turn means that inflation hikes arising from excessive money printing and budget deficits can cause recessions.

In sum, there are three reasons for recessions and rising joblessness—the growing wage gap, soaring oil prices, and high inflation. Of these, the increasing wage gap has been the frequent culprit, occasionally followed by spikes in the prices of oil and other raw materials that lead to high inflation.

CHAPTER 6

BUBBLES ARE TROUBLES

RECENT AMERICAN ECONOMIC HISTORY MAY BE ANALYTICALLY DIVIDED INTO two parts—pre-1980 and post-1980. The main feature that separates these time periods is the level of federal debt. Until 1980 the debt could be measured in billions, but following that year it was better presented in trillions. Furthermore, stock market bubbles and crashes became more frequent in the post-1980 zone; in fact, the worst-ever market collapse occurred in October 1987, when the Dow plummeted 22.5 percent in one day, whereas there was only one major crash in the early 20th century, that of 1929, which was mild in comparison. Another market collapse occurred from 2000 to 2003, and yet another in 2008. Is there any link among debt, bubbles, and crashes? This is the question we now explore.

The new millennium is unique in this respect. In just two decades, it has witnessed two stock bubbles and crashes. So what is a bubble? When the price of an asset climbs much faster than the rest of the economy, a bubble is said to develop. Bubbles are sometimes called manias, during which speculation runs wild and the law of demand breaks down. Normally, you buy less of something as its price rises, but if for some reason you buy more, then your behavior contradicts this law. During the 1990s, for instance, people bought more company shares as their prices increased. Thus rising prices did not curb the public appetite for stocks. That is what happens before an asset bubble is formed. Historically, the asset appreciation has to occur over five or more years before it qualifies as a speculative binge.

If the rupture of a mania were not painful, we could neglect the subject and its underlying causes. But few bubbles have been benign; when they puncture, they leave behind a long trail of bankruptcies, broken homes, crime, unemployment, and starvation; not just the speculators but the entire society suffers with them. That is why speculation should be nipped in the bud, before it surges out of control.

MARKET VERSUS POLICY BUBBLES

There is a major difference between recent manias and those in the 19th and early 20th centuries. The recent bubbles have lasted somewhat longer than those in the past. Back then a bubble would endure no longer than seven years. For instance, the one in the 1920s started in 1922 and ruptured seven years later in 1929, whereas the market mania of the 1990s began to form in 1982, when the Dow averaged 804, and burst in 2000. A crash did occur in 1987, but the Dow resumed its uptrend the next year and reached 11,723 in January 2000. Look at it this way: The Dow was first computed in 1885 and took about 100 years before vaulting past 1,000, in November 1982. Even including the Roaring Twenties, the Dow needed almost a full century to cross the 1,000-point milestone; yet in just 18 years, following 1982, it surged past 11,000. So why have recent bubbles been longer and bigger than ever before?

There are two types of manias: one generated by market forces and another induced by official policy. A market bubble is one that stems from the initiative of the private sector. For some reason a few people become lucky and reap big capital gains from the sale of some asset, and if that asset continues to outperform others, a bubble begins to form in that area. Then other professionals enter that market, and if money keeps flowing in, their success infects the public at large. Since nothing succeeds like success, market optimism is so great toward the end of that boom that it defies gravity. The blind follow the blind and valuations hit the sky, far surpassing the norm. However, every bubble collapses eventually, and then reality sets in; at that point, the new normal reverts to the old norm.

A prerequisite for a market mania is the abundance of cheap credit. When investors make quick bucks, bankers and brokers also pitch in. They fuel the frenzy while making millions themselves. The mania crashes when credit is no longer available.

A policy-induced bubble, on the other hand, may be initiated by private sources but is fed by governing institutions. The government's budget deficit and/or the nation's central bank may provide fodder to the mania. Market-oriented bubbles usually rupture within seven years of their start, but a policy-induced bubble can go on indefinitely, until there is total collapse.

THE WAGE GAP AND BUBBLES

Let us now examine the fundamental cause of an asset bubble. In the preceding chapter we explored the theory of the wage gap and showed that when productivity rises faster than the real wage, the wage gap rises and causes overproduction, which then leads to layoffs. However, if excess production is averted through a rise in consumer and/or government debt, then profits jump faster than GDP. This rise in profit generates a rise in share prices and in turn lays the foundation for a share-market bubble.

Let us now see how profits react to an official policy of low interest rates that stimulate consumer borrowing. There are two main types of incomes in any economy—asset income and wages. National income approximates the value of goods sold, which in turn equals total demand. Asset income derives from people's ownership of stocks, bonds, real estate, and savings, and it accrues chiefly to the top 1 percent of society. The other 99 percent live mostly on their wages. For analytical convenience or simplicity let us assume that asset income equals profits, which, in any case, are the chief source of such income, and consumer spending equals wages. Since income springs from output, then as an approximation[1]

Output = National Income = Profits + Wages

or

Profits = Output − Wages

As a reminder, all the values in an equation are in real or inflation-adjusted terms.

However, if some goods remain unsold, then their value should be deducted from profits, so that

Profits = Output − Wages − Unsold Goods

For instance, if GM produces 20 cars in a quarter and sells only 15 at a price of $10 each, then its sales are $150, and GM's profit is smaller by $50. In the next quarter the company will produce only 15 autos. Initially, suppose the economy is in balance and there is no debt of any type. In other words, in view of the example in chapter 5,

Supply = Demand = $1,000 = Consumer Spending + Investment = $800 + $200

Please note that supply and output are the same thing. In view of our assumption that workers spend everything they earn, consumer spending equals wages, which—with most families living from paycheck to paycheck—is true nowadays, so that

Wages = $800

and

Profits = Output − Wages = $1,000 − $800 = $200

Let wages decline by $100. So

Demand = $700 + $200 = $900

Do profits rise? No. This is because sales have also fallen by $100. As wages decline, workers buy less than before, and layoffs follow almost immediately. If the Federal Reserve responds with sufficiently low interest rates, then consumers borrow money, and if this borrowing matches the fall in consumer spending, then

Demand = Wages + Consumer Borrowing + Investment = $700 + $200 + $100 = $1,000 = Supply

Here the economy is in balance again, and those fired are called back to work, but see what happens to profits now:

Profits = Output − Wages = $1,000 − $700 = $300

So profits jump by $100, because unsold goods vanish. In the absence of consumer borrowing, profits were constant, but now they soar, because every dollar of consumer borrowing has gone into profits. This explains why the one-percenters have been getting wealthier since 2009 even though wages and family income have been declining or stagnant. With soaring profits, no wonder the stock market had a 28 percent return in 2013.

Let me repeat the argument for further clarity. As the wage gap rises, from either a fall in the wage rate or a rise in productivity, supply exceeds demand. There is overproduction and profits may actually fall. But if consumer borrowing resulting from the drop in interest rates absorbs the unsold goods, business revenue rises by the amount of that borrowing, and with wage costs staying constant or falling, the entire debt goes into raising profits.

Any kind of borrowing raises profits by the same amount, provided the nation is not in a serious recession. If consumers are unable to borrow all $100 to match the value of unsold goods, then the government pitches in by raising its budget deficit by the needed amount to maintain a balance in the economy. The point is that the monopoly capitalist always benefits hugely from the so-called monetary and fiscal policies. These are not policies but actually WMEs, or weapons of mass exploitation, because they create the false impression that the government is doing something for those laid off. The elected officials are simply trying to preserve their own jobs and corporate profits. Workers are indeed called back to work, but only at lower wages.

Thus, the end result is exactly the same if productivity increases, and wages don't, or if productivity rises faster than the real wage. Profits climb quickly only if the rising wage gap is accompanied by a sufficient rise in debt. If this process continues for years, profits keep growing faster than GDP, and a stock market bubble is inevitably born. A bubble in one asset normally inspires a bubble in another, as realized capital gains in one market are invested in another. This is why share-market gains are normally associated with gains in real estate. This happened in the 1920s and then again from 2000 to 2007. The stock market did crash in 2000 but regained its footing by 2002 and then, fueled by low interest rates, resumed its upward march. Low interest rates along with hefty capital gains then gave rise to an unprecedented housing bubble.

There is another reason why share prices respond positively to low interest rates. Other financial instruments, such as bonds, become less attractive because of their reduced yield, so that stocks become more attractive. But the main impetus comes from the rise in the wage gap, which forces the government to adopt debt-creating policies. If productivity and wages rise in the same proportion, profits will still rise, but only in proportion to GDP growth. Share prices will then climb at the rate of productivity growth, but there will be no bubble. *Thus bubbles are usually born in weaker economies, in which wages trail productivity.*

Why do all bubbles eventually burst? Every speculative binge sows the seeds for its own destruction. Banks giveth and banks taketh away. Unfortunately for the borrowers, lenders normally require good collateral for their loans, unless, of course, the lender is our Federal Reserve or the European Central Bank (ECB), both of which have been throwing good money after bad since 2008, to bail out financial institutions, regardless of the consequences. Their misguided actions again spawned bubbles in share and oil markets, and expensive oil does not help the cause of job creation. The ECB even bailed out sovereign nations such as Greece, Spain, and Italy, but all this has done is buy some time. The wage gap in Europe continues to be high, and unless this gap is brought down through proper policy, the eurozone's joblessness will stay high.

Banks contribute to asset bubbles and then help them burst as well. A time comes when consumers run out of good collateral; at that point, banks curtail their lending, and, as consumer borrowing drops, supply exceeds demand, and layoffs immediately follow. One round of firings leads to another, because the unemployed trim their spending further, and everything begins to unravel. All bubbles rupture almost simultaneously, and what could have been a minor recession turns into a mega-recession or depression. Usually the real estate binge is the first to puncture, followed by oil and stock manias.

As some employed homeowners are fired, they are unable to pay their monthly mortgages. This culminates in a full-blown banking crisis, as some lenders begin to lose money, and induces governments to bail out financial institutions. Experts are quick to blame the escalating catastrophe on what they see with their own eyes, but the real cause is hidden behind the scenes. It lies in the relentless rise in the wage gap that various administrations tolerated, nay promoted, in the past to please the oligarchs, and in the frenzied indebtedness that the government imposed on the system to postpone the problem of layoffs.

As bank lending and consumer borrowing decline, panicky officials, in their ignorance, look for the same old medicine that precipitated the crisis. Unwilling to confront the oligarchs, they waste taxpayers' money even more. Federal debt rises in a crescendo and stabilizes joblessness, but until the wage gap returns to precrisis levels, debt creation can only postpone the malady.

Let us see why the government debt soars soon after bubbles burst. We have seen above that in the modern world, the economic balance of supply and demand prevails only if

Unsold Goods = Consumer Borrowing + Budget Deficit

Suppose unsold goods equal $200, consumer borrowing equals $150, and the budget deficit equals $50. In this case, the economy is in balance and there are no layoffs. Now suppose banks trim their lending and consumer borrowing falls by $20; then the deficit must rise by the same amount to avoid layoffs; say it increases only $5. Then unsold goods exceed total borrowing, and some people are fired. Rising unemployment leads to a further decline in consumer borrowing, and more layoffs follow. This way the deficit has to rocket to make up for the continued fall in consumer credit. Tax receipts also plunge, while unemployment benefits soar. So, for a while, layoffs may mount in spite of the soaring deficit and federal debt.

The arguments presented above find plentiful support from economic history. It is well-known that consumer debt soared during the 1920s—from about 3 percent of GDP in 1919 to about 7 percent in 1929—while the government budget had a slight surplus. Did the wage gap rise? Yes, it did. Thus, the ground was fertile for share prices to soar, and that is exactly what transpired. Figure 6.1 illustrates the point that both the wage gap in manufacturing industries—for which the data are available—and the overall debt rose sharply during the 1920s, because consumer credit jumped while the

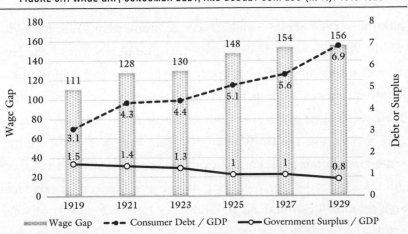

FIGURE 6.1: WAGE GAP, CONSUMER DEBT, AND BUDGET SURPLUS (IN %): 1919–1929

Source: Historical Statistics of the United States, *Series D68, D727, and D802.*

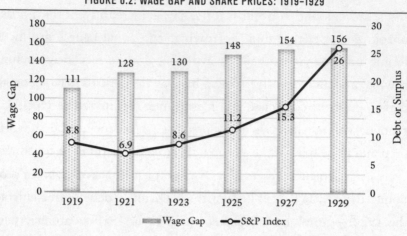

FIGURE 6.2: WAGE GAP AND SHARE PRICES: 1919-1929

Source: Historical Statistics of the United States, *Series X495.*

government budget surplus slowly declined. The combination of the growing wage gap and debt then led to a sharp rise in the S&P stock index, as revealed by figure 6.2.

US ECONOMY: 1962-2012

Now let's take a close look at US economic behavior following World War II, when budget surpluses practically vanished. Here again we find substantial support for the wage-gap hypothesis illustrated above. Table 6.1 presents data over five decades, from 1962 to 2012. It displays various credit or debt measures that, our theory says, are positively related to the wage gap, which is presented in column 5. Column 2 examines consumer borrowing, column 3 shows the borrowing or debt by the federal government, and column 4 is obtained by adding columns 2 and 3; all these are values expressed as percentages of GDP. We should focus on the aggregate debt measure displayed by column 4, because that is what absorbs unsold goods. The table shows that the wage gap was virtually constant during the 1960s but rose slightly in the 1970s; not surprisingly, aggregate debt did not rise, and in fact declined. This is because there was no need to fight large-scale unemployment. Federal debt actually fell as the government retired some of its debt accumulated in World War II, while consumers refrained from excessive borrowing.

The table reveals that there was not much of a trend in consumer credit between 1962 and 1980, but that later it began a steady rise for nearly two decades, peaking in 2000 at 17 percent. The federal debt relative to GDP decreased from 1962 to 1980 but then began to rise, as did the aggregate level of consumer and federal debt. Thus, after 1980 all types of debt measures generally exhibited a rise. The measure that is most significant is displayed in column 4, revealing a steady increase since that year. The reason for this lies in the relentless rise in the wage gap. What happened? There was a remarkable change in federal policy after 1980, as so-called supply-side economics came to dominate government thinking. Regressive taxation,

TABLE 6.1: WAGE GAP AND GDP SHARES OF CONSUMER CREDIT AND
FEDERAL DEBT IN THE UNITED STATES (IN %): 1962–2012

(1)	(2)	(3)	(4)	(5)
	Consumer	Federal	Consumer +	
Year	Credit	Debt	Federal Debt	Wage Gap
1962	12	53	65	72
1970	13	38	51	74
1980	13	33	46	77
1990	14	56	70	86
1999	14	55	69	86
2000	17	57	74	88
2010	17	94	111	94
2012	16	105	121	95

Source: Council of Economic Advisers, The Economic Report of the President, *2012,* B-1, B-77, B-79.

which hurts low-income groups, took over as the income tax rates fell for individuals and corporations, while other tax rates, which burden the middle class, went up. As argued in the next chapter, all the reasons that produce a rise in the wage gap came into full swing, and, not surprisingly, aggregate debt soared.

The 1980s were the early and formative years of the bubble economy, which arrived after the recession of 1990. Share prices began to surge after 1982, but the public obsession with the stock market began only after the Gulf War in early 1991. America's easy victory over Iraq in the war, along with the concurrent fall of Soviet communism, created a general aura of optimism, and share markets not only took off but also found enthusiastic public support.

However, this prosperity was built on the sandy foundation of debt, which, as column 4 shows, rose steadily after 1980. In 1999 something occurred that had not happened since 1969: the federal government had a surplus in its budget, so that government borrowing as well as debt growth actually fell.

The wage-gap theory says that when debt growth slows down, the demand-supply gap comes to the surface. This is precisely what happened in 1999, as aggregate debt as a percentage of GDP tumbled. Then it took just a few months before the share markets peaked—the Dow in January 2000 and the Nasdaq index in March 2000—only to crash soon after. The decline in debt growth resulted in overproduction and a fall in profits. Consequently, the Nasdaq composite index tumbled from a high of 5,049, reached on March 9, 2000, all the way to about 1,180 in September 2001, or by 75 percent, whereas the Dow fell from 11,700 to as low as 7,200, or by 39 percent.

In the aftermath of a crash come recession and stagnation—even depression. What is the difference between a recession and a depression? President Reagan once remarked, "Recession is when a neighbor loses his job. Depression is when you lose yours." There is a large grain of truth and wisdom in what the president said. The extent of joblessness is precisely what should define when a slump begins and when it ends. During the 19th century the level and duration of un-employment defined several depressions, in each of which joblessness lasted five to seven years. In terms of Mr. Reagan's quip, the Great Recession was actually a depression, because high unemployment persisted longer than six years.

At the start of 2007 there was a tenuous balance between sup-ply and demand, as consumer and government borrowing was large enough to absorb unsold goods. By midyear the housing bubble began to burst, leading some panicky banks to trim their lending, which in turn led to a jump in unsold goods and overproduction. By December companies began to lay off workers, and the debt-built economy started to unravel. As fired workers filed for unemploy-ment benefits, government spending and deficit went up further, but layoffs continued to mount. After all, politicians had been postponing joblessness ever since 1980 by means of debt creation or so-called monetary and fiscal policies. By 2007 the wage gap had risen so much that borrowing was not high enough to prevent overproduction.

The federal deficit was just $161 billion in 2007 but climbed to $457 billion in 2008; however, since consumer credit failed to grow, overproduction and thus layoffs increased. Consumer credit fell the next year; naturally the federal deficit shot up to $1.4 trillion. In spite of the gargantuan deficit, over eight million people were laid off in 2008 and 2009.

In retrospect, the giant increase in the deficit occurred because the government needed to make up for the shortfall in consumer borrowing in order to minimize overproduction. After 2010 con-sumer borrowing picked up somewhat, and then the deficit began to decline. All told, by 2014, in a matter of 14 years, the federal debt had rocketed to $17.8 trillion from just $5.5 trillion at the start of the new millennium. Such was the carnage of market bubbles and crashes, and the official economic policies that initiated and abetted them.

BUBBLE ECONOMY

The phrase "bubble economy" became popular during the 1980s, when Japan experienced stock market euphoria, which at the time appeared to dwarf the corresponding euphoria in the United States. A bubble economy is born when debt, business investment, business mergers, and share prices collectively appear to flout all bounds of rationality. Together they exceed productivity rise and GDP growth. Speculation thrives, as the general public and financial institutions rush to acquire various assets at exorbitant prices.

In Japan, the price of land leaped even faster than share prices. At one point the city of Tokyo's real estate was valued above the real estate in all of California. The only thing that sinks in the bubble economy is sanity—that and the fraction of GDP going into wages and consumption.

The speculative bubble is supported by a mushrooming debt, and common sense tells us that debt cannot rise forever. In such times, experts may come out with various ratios such as the price-earnings ratio, the debt-to-GDP ratio, the debt-to-consumption ratio, and so on, offering pearls of wisdom to assure us that these ratios are reasonable. But rationality dictates that the debt binge must come to a halt someday.

When the public is up to its neck in loans, financial institutions simply slow their lending for fear of defaults by borrowers. Some households and corporations become risky customers. Few mergers are as successful as their organizers had hoped. Companies begin to fail; some file for bankruptcy, and credit growth slows down. This is the beginning of a chain reaction that unravels the bubble economy.

The seed of the speculative bubble is also the seed of its destruction. The rising wage gap feeds profits on one side and debt on the other. A time comes when the debt growth slows. That is when the demand-supply imbalance, thus far masked by growing debt, comes to the surface. That is when profits begin to fall, and the nation receives a sudden jolt. First, the stock market moves sideways. But as excess supply of goods continues, share prices begin to crash.

Most of the investors then head for the exit, in a stampede that cripples mega-fortunes built on the foundation of paper profits or sandy capital gains. Those who were late in joining the bubble party suffer real losses; some even lose their retirement money and lifetime savings.

That is why governments should do all they can to suppress a speculative bubble. Capital gains may come and go, but debt is there forever, until it is paid off or until the debtor declares bankruptcy, neither of which is a happy prospect.

THE WAGE GAP IN JAPAN

Does the wage-gap thesis apply to other countries as well? It is based purely on common sense and thus has universal validity. Let's see whether it applies to Japan, which developed a bubble economy in the 1980s.

Japan's economic progress is truly a Cinderella story. With the nation having risen from the devastation caused by World War II, Japan's economic growth is often described as miraculous. You will now see that the Japanese miracle occurred when the nation's wage gap was more or less constant, and troubles began when the gap started to increase. From 1950 to 1970, real GDP grew above the rate of 10 percent per year, a feat rarely matched by other nations. Reliable data about wages and productivity start from the 1960s, and that is where our analysis picks up.

Take a look at table 6.2, which presents indexes for real wages, productivity, and the wage gap from 1965 to 1997. The real wage index, before taxes, increased from 32 in 1965 to 73 in 1975, a climb of 128 percent. Similarly, manufacturing productivity rocketed from 21 to 51, or by 143 percent. In other words, the real wage kept pace with productivity gains.

TABLE 6.2: INDEXES OF WAGE GAP AND SHARE PRICES IN JAPAN: 1965–1997

(1) Year	(2) Real Wage	(3) Productivity	(4) Wage Gap (in %)	(5) Share Price Index
1965	32	21	66	9
1970	50	38	76	16
1975	73	51	70	31
1980	75	64	86	48
1985	81	77	95	100
1990	95	95	100	219
1995	107	109	102	100
1997	110	119	109	101

Source: International Comparisons of Manufacturing Productivity and Unit Labor Cost Trends, 1997, *Bureau of Labor Statistics (BLS), US Department of Labor, 1998, and* International Financial Statistics, *various issues, The International Monetary Fund (IMF), Washington, DC; Batra,* Crash of the Millennium, *p. 85.*

The numerical illustrations presented above show that an economy's expansion path is smooth when its real wage moves in sync with labor productivity. The early post–World War II Japan is a sterling example of such a smoothly functioning and prospering economy. Its affluence derives primarily from the relative stability of its wage-gap index, which was 66 in 1965 and 70 in 1975. This index is obtained by dividing column 3 by column 2 and then multiplying by 100 to express it as a percentage.

The wage gap actually climbed somewhat, but the rise was meager, given that the hourly output in manufacturing more than doubled between 1965 and 1975 (see column 3). With wages nearly keeping up with productivity, demand kept pace with supply. As a result the country needed little rise in consumer or government debt to cope with soaring output.

Here's a clear-cut example of how wages are the main source of demand, productivity is the main source of supply, and if the two grow proportionately together the macro economy expands smoothly over time, without a prop from public borrowing. From 1960 to 1975, consumer debt was absent, while the government budget and foreign trade were practically in balance.

After 1975, however, some institutional changes, such as the decline in competition, feeble unions, and so on, which had been in the making for some time, began to raise the wage gap. Japanese life would no longer be the same. First came the culture of budget deficits. As Japan's wage gap rose, demand fell relative to supply. The rising government deficit was one way to plug this shortfall; another was to adopt the mercantilist policy of generating surpluses in foreign trade, which required domestic overproduction to be shipped abroad. This way Japan became dependent on foreign markets.

A growing wage gap inevitably generates a speculative bubble in share markets, which in turn may spawn bubbles in other assets such as real estate and precious metals. This is what happened in Japan. Between 1965 and 1975, when wages kept pace with soaring productivity, the index of share prices tripled (see column 5). (This index is compiled by the International Monetary Fund and is different from the well-known Nikkei index, which underlies the IMF estimate.) Stock markets surged but so did manufacturing productivity. This was no speculation or market mania, as booming share prices simply reflected a booming economy. This was real, not paper, prosperity.

Between 1975 and 1990, however, the wage-gap index soared at a rate of 3 percent per year, and the inevitable happened. Stock prices sizzled, with the market index rising by 700 percent over the next 15 years. Between 1975 and 1990, productivity nearly doubled, but share prices surged eightfold. The giant imbalance in the stock markets sparked frenzied speculation in land and housing.

Of course, everyone in Japan celebrated: politicians gloated, financial brokers danced in ecstasy, historians sang hymns of Japanese glory, and prudence disappeared. But then came 1990, the year of reckoning, when the share-price index peaked at 219. First share prices crashed, followed in turn by real estate markets, consumer confidence, and business investment. With them came soaring bankruptcies, shattered families, and, above all, the highest rate of unemployment ever recorded in Japan. By 1997 the Tokyo stock market had plunged an inconceivable, and inconsolable, 55 percent from its peak.

TABLE 6.3: WAGE GAP, DEBT, AND SHARE PRICES IN JAPAN: 2000–2011

Year	Wage Gap (in %)	Debt Share	Share Prices (Nikkei Index)
2000	102	141	18,934
2005	124	180	11,489
2010	149	210	10,546
2011	141	215	10,229

Source: International Comparisons of Manufacturing Productivity and Unit Labor Cost Trends, *Bureau of Labor Statistics (BLS), US Department of Labor, 2013; OECD, iLibrary.org; 1stock1.com.*

More than two decades have passed since the rupture of the bubble, yet Japan is still hobbled by stagnation and gloom. Such are the ultimate consequences of the growing wage gap.

Like much of the world, the Japanese were looking forward to better days in the new millennium. Unfortunately, what they got was more of the same, as shown in table 6.3. First and foremost, the wage gap continued to rise, and so did government debt as a percentage of GDP. As for share prices, they continued their fall. The Nikkei index could never recover its glorious past. It had peaked at the end of 1989 at close to 39,000, and at the start of the new millennium it was down to about 19,000. The global share price crash from 2000 to 2003 infected the Tokyo index as well, and all Japan could do was to stem the rout by raising its debt further. The economy began to recover in 2004, only to face another crisis in 2007, which meant another round of a rise in national debt. Japan offers a precious lesson to the world in terms of what works and what does not in developing an economy from scratch.

THE WAGE GAP IN GERMANY

If Japan was the lion of Asia, Germany was and is the tiger of Europe. World War II destroyed both countries, but both astounded the world with their accomplishments. Germany is regarded as the locomotive that pulls Europe. Its economy is the largest in the continent and the fourth-largest in the world.

TABLE 6.4: INDEXES OF WAGE GAP, PER-CAPITA GDP, AND SHARE PRICES IN GERMANY: 1960–1995*

(1) Year	(2) Wage Gap (%)	(3) Per-Capita GDP	(4) Share Price Index
1960	106	17,440	34
1965	101	20,650	28
1970	96	24,660	29
1975	93	26,870	29
1980	90	31,620	31
1985	96	33,800	68
1990	90	30,590	100
1995	91	35,710	103

*After 1990 the figures are for unified Germany.

Source: International Comparisons of Manufacturing Productivity and Unit Labor Cost Trends, 2013, Bureau of Labor Statistics, US Department of Labor, and International Financial Statistics, various issues; Batra, Crash of the Millennium, p. 96.

Germany's economic growth has been unique in terms of its wage gains. As revealed by table 6.4, the wage-gap index fell steadily for German workers over the 20 years from 1960 to 1980. The fruit of productivity growth accrued mostly to workers because of the presence of powerful unions. In this respect, Germany offers a sharp contrast to virtually all other nations, where the wage gap seldom fell. It set an example for all others interested in transforming the poor into a thriving middle class.

Let's see what the wage-gap decline generated in Germany. First, there was no need for consumers to go into debt, which was near zero for a long time. Similarly, budget deficits at the state and federal levels were absent. Corporations, also, were mostly free from debt. The falling wage gap made all this possible.

Neoclassical economists argue that rising wages hurt business investment as well as employment. They oppose increasing the minimum wage, which they say ends up harming the unskilled worker by forcing him into leisure, which is their euphemism for joblessness. This is a self-serving argument, because it tends to enrich the rich, who finance such research through lucrative gifts and grants. Germany's swift progress following World War II clearly belies the neoclassical dogma, which has been a standard menu in almost every principles text used around the world.

Normally, it is not easy to find a straightforward link between the wage gap and the rate of unemployment, because joblessness can be postponed by the expansion of money supply and government debt. However, such is not the case with Germany. This is because the nation not only shunned budget deficits but also tightly controlled the money-printing press to avert inflation. Figure 6.3 shows that as the German wage gap fell, so did its rate of unemployment.

In fact, from 1960 to 1970, as the wage-gap index declined from 106 to 96, the rate of unemployment was below 1 percent in Germany. Meanwhile, in its neighboring countries, as well as in Canada

FIGURE 6.3: WAGE GAP AND RATE OF UNEMPLOYMENT IN GERMANY: 1960-1970

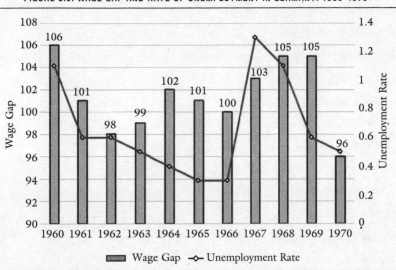

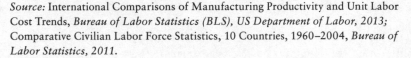

Source: International Comparisons of Manufacturing Productivity and Unit Labor Cost Trends, *Bureau of Labor Statistics (BLS), US Department of Labor, 2013;* Comparative Civilian Labor Force Statistics, 10 Countries, 1960–2004, *Bureau of Labor Statistics, 2011.*

and the United States, the rate was three to ten times as high. So you see, rising salaries for employees create no problems so long as productivity rises as well; in fact, trouble arises when wages fail to keep up with growing efficiency.

The German economy also supports our finding that a growing, or at least constant, wage gap is a necessary condition for a share-price boom. Since the gap declined in the nation from 1960 to 1980, we should expect the stock market to stagnate. Table 6.4 demonstrates that this is precisely what happened. In spite of soaring productivity, the German stock market index actually declined from 34 in 1960 to 31 in 1980. It soared thereafter, as the wage gap began to rise, but another reason for its rise was the booming New York Stock Exchange, which began to pull global share markets with it.

I will have plenty more to write about Germany in subsequent chapters.

CHAPTER 7

MONOPOLY CAPITALISM AND THE RISING WAGE GAP

WITH THE POVERTY RATE AT ITS HIGHEST LEVEL IN MORE THAN 50 YEARS, many people think the United States has already become a nation of haves and have-nots. For the haves, the early 2010s were perhaps the best time in our history, but for the have-nots, circumstances were getting grimmer and grimmer. With budget deficits and money printing at record levels, the wealthy one-percenters enjoyed their routine bonuses and capital gains, while the unemployed were not sure where their next meal would come from. Such are the long-term consequences of the rising wage gap.

What really astounds many is that the average wage has stagnated since 1980 in spite of workers' rising education and efficiency. National output per worker or per hour of work effort is known as the productivity of labor. Because of new investment and technology, labor productivity has increased almost every decade since the birth of the American Republic, in 1789, although its pace of increase has seen ups and downs. The amount by which hourly output rises from one year to the next is called the rate of productivity growth. This rate has varied over time, but its direction has been generally positive.

Fairness and common sense demand that wages keep pace with productivity. Everyone expects to be compensated for their hard work and merit, and this rule held up well for much of American history. In a healthy economy, the wage gap is low and constant, so that the real wage keeps up with efficiency gains. Otherwise the gap rises and tends to generate all sorts of unexpected events in society, because whenever it rises persistently, the macro economy turns topsy-turvy. Business activity zooms at first and inflates into a bubble, but then calamities follow.

Figure 7.1 displays the behavior of the real wage and productivity from 1869 to 1959, showing that normally the two move in sync with each other. The rising gap between real wages and productivity is not normal for the US economy. Almost a century of data reveal that real wages in the United States went up every decade with growing productivity, and the wage-gap index moved little except during wars or depressions. Thus, the figure displays the generally positive link between real wages and productivity. Reliable productivity figures go as far back as 1869, and earnings figures are available from 1860 on. However, for both entities our graph begins with 1869 to see if any association exists between them.

The lower track of the graph displays the index of overall productivity with a base year of 1958, whereas the upper path depicts the index of real annual earnings of nonfarm employees with the base year of 1914. The base year in economics is used as a year of comparison and is selected to eliminate the effect of inflation. The bases are not the same because the two series were generated by different writers. That, however, makes no difference, because we seek to see how wages and productivity behave over time.

The two tracks in the graph are almost parallel, indicating a one-to-one connection between real earnings and productivity. The productivity index rose from 15 in 1869 to 27 in 1899 and 104 in 1959, whereas real earnings jumped from $380 to $563 and then to $1,701. Thus productivity and nonfarm wages generally kept pace with each other.

FIGURE 7.1: LABOR PRODUCTIVITY AND REAL WAGES IN THE UNITED STATES: 1869–1959

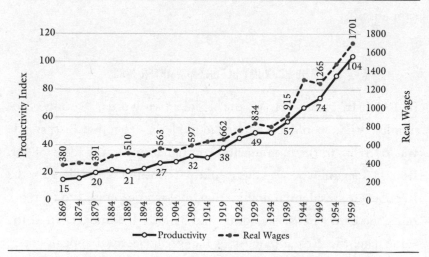

Source: Historical Statistics of the United States, *Series D683, D726, and D736.*

Even after 1959 real wages and hourly output moved closely together. This is not depicted in figure 7.1 but is demonstrated in the preceding chapter. As shown in chapter 6, the wage gap was more or less constant between 1962 and 1975 but grew quickly after 1980. Chapter 6 relies on data from the *Economic Report of the President*, starting from 1962. Relevant figures are also available from a different study done by the Bureau of Labor Statistics (BLS) starting from 1950, but that study uses a different base year. It turns out that from 1950 to 1961, the wage-gap index actually fell. This segment of US economic history is unique and will be analyzed in detail in chapter 9. Thus we see that for more than a century, from 1869 to 1975, as far back as the data permit, US real wages kept up with productivity, even during the Great Depression, with the singular exception of a short period in the 1940s, when World War II distorted the landscape of the economy. Unfortunately, following 1980 that exception was repeated in peacetime, year after year. Thus something unprecedented in the American chronicle must have happened around that pivotal year; the question is what. The answer comes from monopoly capitalism.

THE ECONOMY BEFORE AND AFTER 1980

In 1980 Mr. George H. W. Bush spoke two words, "voodoo economics," that would become memorable in economic history. He was referring to the monumental contradictions in the ideas of Mr. Ronald Reagan, who was then—like Mr. Bush—a candidate for the Republican presidential nomination, and who promised to trim tax rates, increase defense spending, and balance the budget, all at the same time. Mr. Reagan's message had great electoral appeal; voters were charmed by the idea of having their cake and eating it too. Not surprisingly Mr. Reagan, along with a contrite Mr. Bush as his running mate, won handily over an unpopular Democrat, Mr. Jimmy Carter.

The rest, as they say, is history. Soon after his inauguration in 1981, President Reagan got his tax cuts and a large increase in the military budget; while tax rates were slashed for people in all income brackets, the wealthiest received the lion's share of the windfall. Corporations were also amply rewarded, not only with cuts in corporate taxes but also with hefty defense contracts. The president fulfilled his promise, but his eloquence was unable to bend mathematical logic. The federal deficit, instead of vanishing like a vapor, climbed first to a record $100 billion, then to $150 billion and finally to $221 billion, all within a year.

Now the president faced a major problem. How do you finance these unprecedented deficits? He resorted to what he called "revenue enhancements." In 1982 he raised the gasoline tax and the excise tax, which is a federal sales tax. Yet the deficit failed to budge, because these changes generated paltry revenue. For some mysterious reason, he did not want to touch the revenue enhancements that benefited the oligarchs, who by then had become his ardent supporters. His adviser, Mr. Alan Greenspan, as the chairman of a commission on Social Security, then came up with an artful stratagem.

One fine morning in 1982, Mr. Greenspan told the nation that the Social Security retirement fund was nearly empty and needed a large infusion of money to keep it solvent over the next 50 years. One way to keep the retirement system viable was to sharply raise the Social Security tax and the self-employment tax. This way the fund would have a savings account of sorts, and the revenue, along with its interest income, would be enough to secure the pension benefits of retirees in the future. The commission in effect promised workers that their higher tax burden would guarantee their retirement benefits.

Both Republicans and Democrats, along with the president, hastened to accept Greenspan's proposals. Without enough hearings from affected parties, Congress enacted a law in 1983 to raise these levies. The self-employment tax, which imposes a huge burden on small businesses, jumped 66 percent. Since 1984, when the new law went into effect, the pension fund has collected some $3 trillion worth of extra revenue, including interest.

So how much money is now available in the fund? Nearly zero. Where did that ballyhooed savings account go? Almost all of it went into the pockets of oligarchs, whose tax burden plunged at the expense of the vast majority of people. The cut in income and

corporate taxes caused a horrendous federal deficit, which, contrary
to the promise made by the Greenspan commission, was financed by
payroll tax revenues. Even then the budget could not be balanced.

In spite of the giant tax increases to protect the Social Security
program, US budget deficits continued. The government borrowed
billions, not only from rich Americans but also from rich Japanese,
Canadians, Arabs, Australians, Germans, Mexicans, and even citizens of developing economies. China was not yet involved in this
borrowing spree, but its participation would come in the 1990s and
beyond. As mentioned in previous chapters, so large was the annual
deficit that, in the president's first term alone, the federal debt surpassed the debt accumulated by all the presidents preceding him. By
the end of Reagan's second term, in early 1989, the debt had climbed
to $2.6 trillion; it had reached $5.6 trillion by 2000.

In retrospect, Mr. Reagan's claims and promises aptly deserved
the label of voodoo economics. Harvard professor J. K. Galbraith
eloquently described the accomplishments of the 1980s:

> There have been few periods in American or world history . . .
> that have been more scrupulously examined from an economic
> and social viewpoint than the 1980s. Much of the resulting
> judgment, though to be sure not all, has been unfavorable. Tax
> reduction oriented to the affluent, unduly enhanced defense ex-
> penditures and a large deficit in the federal budget were the
> prize manifestations of error. Related was the large and per-
> sistent deficit in the American balance-of-payments account,
> causing the United States to shift from being the world's largest
> creditor to being, by a wide margin, its largest debtor.[1]

Evidently something happened after 1980 that changed the course
of the American economy forever. Gone were the relatively low budget deficits, respectable rates of saving and GDP growth, balanced

international trade, practically zero foreign debt, relatively low income and wealth disparity, and sizable middle class. All this slowly but surely vanished after 1980. What diabolical thing happened? It is the so-called supply-side economics that, despite the carnage it has rendered, still rules economic thought. This theory is so obviously deceptive and self-serving that it deserves no comment, but, because of its ubiquity, it must be examined and exposed.

According to the theory, low income tax rates on high earnings offer an incentive to save, work hard, and invest; they stimulate economic growth and generate revenue high enough to balance the federal budget. This idea became so commonplace that a front-page article in the *Wall Street Journal* made copious reference to it.[2] Although the doctrine seems designed mainly to further the interests of millionaires whose tax bill is large, it has been the cornerstone of economic policy for a long time.

Before we look at history to examine the theory's validity, let us see if the idea makes any sense. People's incentive to work hard comes from their desire to eat, live in houses, receive education and health care, and meet the needs of their families. If the income tax rate goes up, few will stop working or trim their work effort, unless they are independently wealthy. An exceptionally small minority of the fabulously rich may need an incentive to work diligently, but not someone who is poor or belongs to the middle class.

Even those with above-average incomes generally feel the need to work hard to maintain their lifestyles. Furthermore, if you lower the income tax rate for the affluent, then you have to rely on regressive taxation, which raises taxes on the (smaller) earnings of the poor and the middle class, because the government cannot run on air. The supply-side idea is thus one-sided, ignores the state's need for revenue, resorts to exceptions, and is yet offered as a thesis applying to everyone. Isn't it interesting that the theory seeks to trim only the income tax, not other levies.

Let us now look at some facts, which are presented in a series of self-explanatory graphs. The income tax rates were slashed in 1981 for individuals and corporations to fulfill the promises made by the theory. Did those promises prevail?

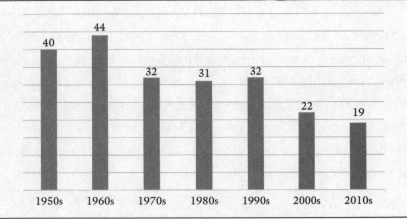

Source: Council of Economic Advisers, The Economic Report of the President, *various issues.*

HIGH GROWTH WITH HIGH INCOME TAXES

History thoroughly contradicts the low-income-tax theology. All you need to debunk its validity is one readily available fact: *During the 1950s and '60s, economic growth was much stronger than in the 1980s and '90s, even though the marginal income tax rate on top-earning families, less than 40 percent today, was as high as 91 percent in the past.* Anyone earning more than $200,000, equivalent to $2 million today, had to pay this rate. In other words, when millionaires paid as much as 91 cents out of their earnings above $2 million, economic growth was much stronger than that observed since 1980, as is displayed by figure 7.2.

There were some tax loopholes, and most people escaped the bite of the top rate. But even the effective rate, according to the IRS, was no less than 75 percent. Real GDP grew by 40 percent in the 1950s, 44 percent in the 1960s, and 32 percent in the 1970s, compared with a mere 31 percent in the 1980s and 32 percent in the 1990s. Yet the top tax rate was 50 percent in the first half of the 1980s and just 28 percent in the second half, 70 percent in the 1970s, 80 percent in the 1960s, and an unbelievable 91 percent in the 1950s. And in the new millennium, economic growth has shriveled further. It may be noted that the low growth rate of the 1970s arose mostly from a huge jump in the price of oil engineered by OPEC; still, that rate matched or exceeded what followed in the coming decades. Observed facts blatantly contradict the view that high income taxes hurt economic growth. Yet politicians today, backed by most economists, ardently preach this dogma. These facts are undisputed and easily accessible from annual issues of *The Economic Report of the President* itself.

FIGURE 7.3: PERSONAL RATE OF SAVING IN THE UNITED STATES (IN %): 1960–2014

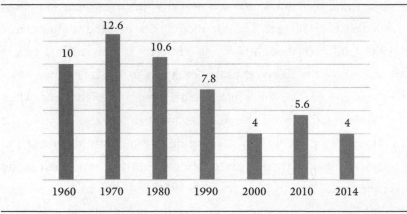

Source: Federal Reserve Economic Data, or Federal Reserve Bank, St. Louis, 2014.

What about the rate of saving? Supply-side theory preached that as people had more money in their pockets from the income tax cut, they would save and invest more, thereby raising the growth rate. See how absurd this idea is. It would have been more credible to say that the rich would save more but that others, facing the higher payroll taxes required to control the budget deficit, would save less, with unpredictable results overall. In reality, savings were decimated, as is clear from figure 7.3. With the vast majority of workers having to pay a gargantuan Social Security tax and higher gasoline and excise taxes, how could middle-class families possibly save more? The personal rate of saving, which until 1980 usually exceeded 10 percent, fell by more than half, to 4 percent, by 2000. It remained close to that rate even in the new millennium.

The supply-side idea also offered another gem, namely, that low corporate and income tax rates stimulate business investment. Figure 7.4 examines this view graphically to see how the investment share of GDP has reacted to changes in the tax code. In 1980 the top tax rate was 70 percent, and business investment equaled 13 percent of GDP. As the rate fell to 50 percent in 1981, the oligarchs received a huge tax break, but did they invest more? No, they spent less on capital formation, because by 1985 the investment share had declined to 12.5 percent. The top income tax rate fell to 28 percent in 1986, and even though it rose slightly to 31 percent in 1990, it was well below the 50 percent rate prevailing in 1981. Did the investment rate go up? No, it fell again—this time to 10.7 percent. Then Mr. William Clinton was elected president in 1992 and raised the tax rate to 39.6 percent. Now, according to the supply-side theorists, investment should have decreased, but the contrary happened, as the investment rate rose to 11 percent in 1995 and then to 12.7 percent in 2000.

In 2001 a Republican, Mr. George W. Bush, became president and revived the supply-side theory; as the top tax rate fell to 34 percent, so did the rate of investment. Thus, whenever the income tax rate has declined, the investment rate has declined with it, thereby revealing the bankruptcy of the supply-side idea. In hindsight, the downward trend in the rate of investment simply reflected the sinking rate of saving. Nor were falling corporate taxes of any help. Figure 7.4 reveals a declining trend in investment share, against the backdrop of a relentless plunge in the share of corporate tax in total federal revenue.

The figure may seem difficult to comprehend, but the main point is clear from the two trend lines that are almost parallel to each other. Falling corporate taxes have gone hand in hand with falling investment, and the reasons are the growing tax burden on the middle class and the rising wage gap.

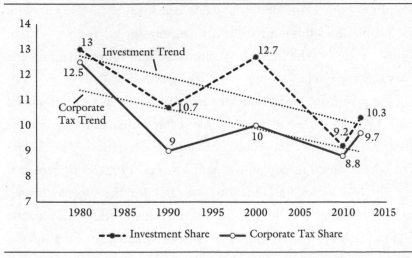

FIGURE 7.4: CORPORATE TAXATION AND GDP SHARE OF INVESTMENT IN THE UNITED STATES (IN %): 1980–2012

Source: *Council of Economic Advisers,* The Economic Report of the President, *2013.*

What is the role of oligarchs in fostering the supply-side idea? I have no eyewitness to prove that they were behind its birth. But there is a well-known idiom: If it walks like a duck and quacks like a duck, then it must be a duck. So, if the idea benefits only the oligarchs, who wholeheartedly support it even as their hirelings sing sweet hymns about it, then they alone likely invented it and paid others to popularize it.

"Supply-side economics" is another phrase for the trickle-down theory, which in one word may be called "tricklism." The theory essentially suggests that as the rich get richer, their prosperity seeps down, drip by drip, to the toiling masses. This view won the heart of monopoly capitalists a long time ago, but it is not fooling Independent voters anymore. During the 1970s, the real wage of production workers, who constitute up to 80 percent of the labor force, began a slow decline. Prosperity no longer trickled down, while the wealthy continued to become wealthier. So some experts renamed tricklism as supply-side economics to present a counter to the popular Keynesian idea of demand-side economics. This is because supply and demand are both easily understandable concepts; they resonate with the people, and linking tricklism to supply served to give it credibility, at least to the Republican electorate and Independent voters. This way the public was duped—once again.

However, the supply-side idea is more dangerous to the middle class than its earlier version, as has been borne out through the bitter experience of the public, because it is unabashed tricklism. The trickle-down theory only sought low taxes for the affluent, but the supply-side dogma lauds low tax rates for the super-rich one-percenters along with high levies for all others. Tricklism suggests that the rich are special and deserve deferential treatment from the rest of us.

During the first half of the 1980s, the top-bracket individual and corporate tax rates plummeted while almost all other federal levies soared to finance the jackpot for the rich. During the second half of the decade, things got even worse. After President Reagan was re-elected, in 1984, the oligarchs realized that their best friend would no longer be in office after his second term. He had already rewarded them handsomely with myriad favors, but, their appetite whetted, they wanted more.

They had not received so much charity from any administration since the 1920s. The government had given them billions in tax breaks and then borrowed billions back from them to finance its budget deficit at double-digit interest rates. From 1981 to 1984 the interest rate on 10-year Treasury bonds varied between 11 and 14 percent. How could they not love the president? Where would you get this much return on gilt-edged securities without taking any risk? For them the deficit was a gravy train. The larger the better! This was better than free lunch. They got money from someone and lent it back at a hefty interest rate. Never mind that according to the supply-side theory, the oligarchs were supposed to invest the tax benefit into the economy to create jobs.

In 1986 they persuaded the president to slash the top tax rate further. The one-percenters were so successful this time that the tax code became perverse. The wealthiest faced a 28 percent rate, while those with lower incomes faced a 33 percent rate. Furthermore, the bottom rate jumped from 11 percent to 15 percent. For the first time in history the top rate fell and the bottom one rose simultaneously. Of course, the president and his cohorts alone could not have accomplished this travesty. It was all signed, sealed, and delivered with the help of Democrats.

As stated above, the supply-side dogma was and is unabashed tricklism, because, in addition to this travesty, the lawmakers chose to tax unemployment benefits. In 1987 a president who would not spare unemployment compensation from taxation called for a cut in the capital gains tax, as if capital gains are not income. According to the Tax Foundation, that tax rate was a measly 15 percent in 1988 and stayed there until 2000. Thus, the tax on capital gains was as low as the bottom income tax rate. Meanwhile, even as most politicians have touted their support for small businesses, since 1990 a small-business person has paid a self-employment tax of 15.3 percent on any income above $400, in addition to the regular income tax. Thus, the self-employment tax alone exceeded the levy on capital gains. What else can you expect in an oligarchy?

This is the ultimate in regressive taxation, and it could not but raise the wage gap.

OLIGARCHY AND THE WAGE GAP

It should be clear by now that the tax churning of the 1980s was a direct hit on the middle class by monopoly capitalism. Retirement trust funds alone ended up losing $3 trillion. But there was severe long-term damage to the economy as well, because the new tax code, along with other government policies cherished by the oligarchs, caused a relentless rise in the wage gap. This is the issue that we now address.

The wage gap rises because of covert or overt actions of monopoly capitalists. Normally, under a Republican administration, their actions become overt, bringing them numerous rewards from the administration in the form of tax breaks, corporate subsidies, or lucrative government contracts. When a Democrat occupies the presidency, they usually act behind the scenes and influence lawmakers through campaign donations or promises of lucrative jobs upon retirement from politics. Prior to World War II the wage gap soared only during the 1920s, when the Republicans were in power; but since 1980 it has risen every decade regardless of who is in office. The American oligarchy is now so pervasive that no party can control it. Lobbyists for monopoly capitalists influence the legislation and at times even write laws, word for word. This way government policy ends up benefiting the oligarchs at the expense of everyone else.

How does the government either restrain wages relative to productivity or enrich the rich? It is easy to see that almost all official

economic measures adopted since 1981 and contained in the following list have devastated the middle class:

1. The income tax cut of 1981, which favored the wealthy but
    made it necessary to raise almost all other federal taxes
    sharply—and was thus paid for mostly by the poor and the
    middle class

2. Failure to enforce antitrust laws, leading to mergers among
    large and profitable firms, which in turn killed high-paying
    jobs in numerous industries

3. Oil-industry mergers that were permitted in the 1990s and
    that kept oil prices high for a long time in the middle of the
    worst slump, or stagnation, since the 1930s

4. Relentless mergers among pharmaceutical and health
    insurance companies, which mean that America now spends
    almost 15 percent of GDP, far more than any other nation,
    on health care that is mediocre by European and Japanese
    standards

5. Unchecked use of outsourcing, which kills high-paying jobs
    in manufacturing and services

6. The practice of ignoring the growth of the trade deficit,
    which has destroyed our manufacturing base

7. The 1999 repeal of the Glass-Steagall Act promoted by
    then treasury secretary Lawrence H. Summers, leading to
    reckless lending by banks and an unprecedented housing
    bubble, which collapsed in 2007 to trigger the ongoing
    slump

8. The Bush tax cuts and bailouts, which further benefited the
    rich while nearly doubling the government debt

9. The decimation of the real minimum wage by President
    Reagan and other Republicans. (In 1981 the hourly
    minimum wage bought $8 worth of goods, compared with

$6 by the end of Reagan's presidency, in early 1989, and
with a mere $5.15 in 2006 under Mr. Bush.)

Judging from this nine-point list, is there any government program
that an oligarch would hate? Asked another way, is there any measure that has helped the middle class? I can't think of any. Thus, ever
since 1981 virtually every government policy that was supposed to
help the people actually ended up hurting them. Mergers, outsourcing, and free trade raise productivity but also lower wages, whereas
the other provisions of the above list directly enrich the wealthy.

The 1981 Tax Cut

Let's examine the process through which official policies helped
raise productivity while keeping wages stagnant. Almost every
question in economics can be answered in terms of the concepts of
supply and demand, and wages are no exception. In general, anything that generates a decline in labor demand or a rise in labor supply leads to a fall in the real wage and a rise in the wage gap. Since
the labor force consists primarily of the poor and the middle class,
anything that raises their tax burden can significantly increase the
labor supply. This is because a big rise in their tax bill crimps their
lifestyle, forcing them to work longer hours. Families may also react by sending two members to work. Payroll taxes soared following the 1981 tax cut and sharply trimmed the after-tax income of
the workers, who responded by working overtime to maintain their
living standard. This raised the supply of labor and resulted in wage
stagnation.

The evidence for this comes from the labor-force participation
rate, which is the proportion of the population engaged in employment. Consider figure 7.5, which shows that the participation rate
rose from about 64 percent in 1980 to 66.5 percent in 1990 and 67

FIGURE 7.5: LABOR FORCE PARTICIPATION RATE IN THE UNITED STATES (IN %): 1980–2012

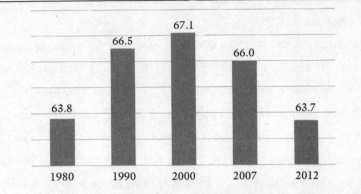

Source: Council of Economic Advisers, The Economic Report of the President, *2014,* B-47.

FIGURE 7.6. OVERTIME HOURS IN THE UNITED STATES (IN %): 1980–2012

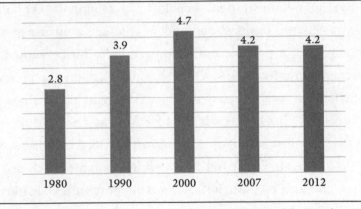

Source: Council of Economic Advisers, The Economic Report of the President, *2014,* B-47.

percent in 2000. By 2012, however, it had plunged to 63.7 percent, but that was the result of a sharp rise in unemployment since 2007. The evidence from overtime work reinforces the message of figure 7.5. Figure 7.6 reveals that overtime hours climbed dramatically after 1980, from 2.8 to 4.7 in 2000, and remained close to that level even in 2012. There is thus plenty of evidence that the tax churning of the 1980s led to a significant jump in labor supply and thus generated wage stagnation.

Another effect of the tax churning was insufficient labor demand. You already know that GDP growth fell in the 1980s and beyond. Millions of people join the labor force every year and look for jobs, which arise from economic expansion. Faltering GDP growth means fewer jobs available to absorb the new job seekers, thereby causing wage stagnation. Thus the tax legislation of the 1980s produced sluggish wages in two ways. First, it raised labor supply; second, it restrained the growth in labor demand relative to new entrants to the jobs market.

Mergers and Acquisitions

The Reagan administration, beholden to monopoly capitalists, was extremely pro-business and seldom enforced antitrust or anti-monopoly laws, a practice that continued even during subsequent Democratic administrations. Officials simply adopted a policy of noninterference with company behavior. The general belief became: what is good for big business is good for America. As a result, business mergers and acquisitions, also known as M&A activity, soared after 1980. An admirable and thorough discussion of such activity has been provided by Piper Jaffray, an economist with USbankcorp, as described in figure 7.7.

Business mergers climbed in the 1920s and then again between 1981 and 2001, crimping rivalry among firms and raising the monopoly power of already oligopolistic industries. In the software industry Microsoft became a giant, as did some pharmaceutical firms in the field of medicine. The 1996 merger between Exxon and Mobil generated a petroleum-industry behemoth with enormous production, profits, and financial clout. Such developments could not

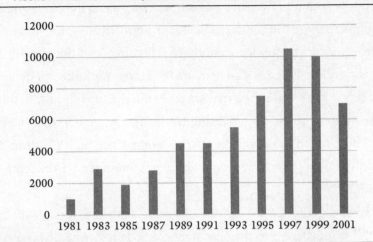

FIGURE 7.7: MERGER AND ACQUISITION DEALS IN THE UNITED STATES: 1981–2001

Source: Piper Jaffray, "US Leveraged Buyout Market 1980–2002," piperjaffray .com.

but raise the wage gap for a variety of reasons. First, merged firms reduce labor demand by immediately laying off some employees. Second, with fewer workers doing the same amount of work, labor efficiency goes up. Both developments cause wages to trail productivity, thereby raising the wage gap.

The Relentless Trade Deficit

Another reason for the growing wage gap is the increasing US reliance on foreign trade. According to the trade-theory literature, globalization—or free trade—tends to raise a country's output per worker, or its productivity. At the same time its real wage falls if it imports labor-intensive products, that is, goods that use a lot of labor to produce a dollar of output. Many American imports such as shoes, textiles, and autos turn out to be labor-intensive relative to American exports such as airplanes, farm goods, and computers.

Rising imports create job losses in import-competing industries, which face competition from abroad, whereas rising exports produce job gains in exporting industries. But if imports are labor-intensive relative to exports, job losses outpace job gains, and the overall impact is a decline in American demand for labor. With the fall in labor demand comes a fall in the real wage, while the overall productivity of the nation rises with increasing trade. The wage gap then has to rise. This pattern has applied to the economy since the 1970s but did not do so during the 1920s, when foreign commerce was exceptionally small.

However, the United States follows a distorted version of free trade. It is indifferent to the persistent trade deficit, whereby imports constantly exceed exports. The idea of free trade originated from a British economist named David Ricardo, who demonstrated numerically that globalization benefits all nations so long as workers are fully employed and exports match imports. This is because exporting industries tend to absorb those laid off from import-competing sectors, so that cheaper imported goods benefit those who remain employed. But when the country has a persistent trade deficit, as we have had since 1980, it is very difficult to maintain full employment, in which case free trade hurts the workers, especially when the trade deficit is with low-wage countries.

There is no other nation that tolerates an import surplus as much as the United States, because such surpluses generates job losses. Then why do we do it? The reason has to do with the oligarchs, who benefit hugely from it. Almost all American oligopolies have moved some of their factories abroad, where wages are low; they want to import as much as possible and sell their goods in the United States, where, because of the lack of competition, they charge high prices. This is a clear-cut recipe to squeeze the middle class. It keeps wages low but profits high. This is another reason why under President Obama the rate of profit neared its all-time high.

Labor Union Decline

Labor unions normally exert a powerful influence on the real wage of their own members. They tend to offset the negative impact of business mergers and the monopoly power of giant firms. But since 1970, union influence, for a variety of reasons, has declined. The real wage of union members suffered as a consequence. However, the result percolated throughout the national labor market, because employers have to pay a wage that competes with the union wage. Otherwise, workers could join the unions, whom producers regard as adversaries. Therefore, when unions lose their influence, the real wage declines in the entire economy, generating a rise in the wage gap. Free trade has a lot to do with the declining power of unions; workers are afraid to unionize, lest their factory moves abroad.

Outsourcing

The most virulent form of free trade is outsourcing, whereby a US firm hires workers in a foreign country to perform tasks that are normally done by American workers. This practice is now a major cause of the soaring wage gap, because it creates double jeopardy for the US economy. On the one hand, demand for labor as well as consumer demand fall as work is outsourced and some workers are laid off, and on the other hand, supply remains constant, so that there is overproduction, which leads to further layoffs and a further decline in the real wage. Thus, outsourcing is now perhaps the biggest cause of stagnation in the US economy.

Let us explore a numerical example. Suppose supply and demand are initially each equal to $1,000, so that there are no layoffs. If 100 workers are employed at an average wage of $8, then each produces $10 worth of output at current prices. If all wages are spent, and investment equals $200, then with a balanced budget and no trade deficit,

Demand = $800 + $200 = Supply

This is an example of a balanced economy. Now suppose that the job of one worker is outsourced. Then employment falls to 99. This is the first negative impact on jobs; but there is the secondary impact as well. If the productivity of the worker hired abroad is the same as that of the US worker, supply remains constant, but US consumer demand falls by $8. So now supply also exceeds demand, and another worker may be fired, or working hours decrease. In this way outsourcing causes double jeopardy for the job market and unemployment.

Deregulation

The banking industry's involvement with speculation was a big reason for the stock market bubble and then the crash in 1929. The Glass-Steagall Act was passed in 1933 to ban this practice, but the law was repealed in 1999. Not surprisingly, speculation surged and bubbles were formed in the housing and oil markets. In 2008 oil hit a record $147 per barrel. As explained in chapter 5, the oil surge also causes double jeopardy, hurting both demand and supply. Labor demand sinks and so does the real wage.

Oil plummeted to nearly $30 per barrel in 2009, but following the Bush bailout, it soon crossed the $100 mark.

The Declining Minimum Wage

The US minimum wage in 2003 was $5.15 and had remained constant since 1997; it rose to $7.25 in 2009. By contrast, the corresponding wage in the late 1960s was close to $10 in terms of 2015 prices. Clearly, the purchasing power of the minimum wage has eroded sharply since 1970. Typically, a minimum-wage employee is a relatively unskilled worker with very little bargaining power. Ten million Americans earn this wage, while another 20 million have their salaries tied directly to it.

The average US wage is far above the minimum. How, then, does the minimum wage affect the average salary? It serves as a benchmark for the salaries of production workers. Both employers and employees look at the minimum wage and add skill-based premiums to it in their own wage negotiations. The greater the skill, the higher the premium.

Thus the benchmark wage sets the standard for the salaries of most nonsupervisory workers, who constitute up to 80 percent of the workforce. When the benchmark declines, naturally production workers experience a drop in the purchasing power of their pay, and the wage gap rises.

Thus, for a wide variety of reasons, the wage gap has risen ceaselessly since 1980, and the end results, as mentioned many times before, are lofty consumer and government debt, hysterical speculation, joblessness, and market crashes.

CHAPTER 8

A TOWN HALL-STYLE DEBATE

BY NOW YOU KNOW WHY THE WAGE GAP HAS BEEN RISING INCESSANTLY since 1980 and how this phenomenon is responsible for virtually all economic ills in the world. What can be done about this? How can we educate the politicians to focus on the fundamentals of supply and demand and their underlying determinants, such as wages and productivity, rather than massive debt creation? This chapter narrates a story about two unemployed workers debating three candidates for the Senate—a Republican, a Democrat, and an Independent—in a town hall setting. It is a fictional story based on the reality of long-term joblessness and poverty.

The unemployed workers are William and Robert, or Bill and Bob. Bill has been a lifelong Democrat, and Bob is a Republican. Both have been in and out of jobs since 1980, when the nation faced a steep recession, similar to—but not as deep as—the one starting in 2007. Bill, with a high school diploma, had his first job as an auto mechanic in 1975, and Bob, a college graduate, started work as the manager of a textile mill in 1978.

The three Senate candidates for the upcoming election in November 2016 are all from Texas. Of them, two are career politicians. Mr. Jonathan Caesar, the incumbent, has been a Republican senator since 1980; he came to office on the long, wide coattails of Mr. Reagan. He is accompanied by his adviser, who is a Nobel Prize winner from the University of Chicago and an Alexander the Great (AG) professor of economics. His challenger, Mr. Samuel Spartacus, has been a House member since 1978 but now has Senate aspirations. Advising him is a Nobel laureate from Harvard University and Napoleon Bonaparte (NB) professor of economics. The third candidate, Mr. Hank Holder, is an Independent. He is a historian with no political experience but has the gall to challenge the big names, as he is tired of the economic and political malaise in the nation and wants to do something about it. He is all by himself.

The prime-time debate has been arranged by Planetary News Network, PNN, and anyone can join the audience. The entire nation is glued to their TV sets because for the first time two jobless workers not only are going to question the candidates about their views on recent government policy, but are also going to talk to their distinguished advisers about what they would do to spur economic growth. Bill and Bob are nervous but well prepared. They have invited questions from the unemployed throughout the world via social media and have made a short list of queries.

Amid loud claps, the PNN host, Mr. David Goliath, enters the hall, followed by the senatorial aspirants and their advisers. He introduces his guests and then asks Bill and Bob to join them on the podium. Bob, the Republican jobless worker, is invited to quiz the candidates for about half an hour.

> Bob: Senator Caesar, I feel honored that you have graciously
>   agreed to answer my queries. I respect you and have voted for
>   you ever since 1980, when you first explained, in layman's

terms, the logic and benevolence of supply-side economics. I started work in 1978 as a manager of a textile firm in Dallas, but was laid off in the recession of 1981, as cheap shirts from Asia flooded our nation. I have a college degree in economics, and learned that free trade is good for all countries. Nevertheless, I contacted your office to complain about the imports, but was told the government offered money to victims of imported goods to retrain into other professions. So I became quiet and worked very hard to understand the workings of another career. Fortunately, in 1982 I found work at Zenith TV, again as a manager. I was happy because I was still a manager and did not have to take a pay cut. I soon forgot my family's trauma.

However, these nasty imports kept coming. In 1990 Zenith closed its doors and fired everyone. I had to get into another retraining program, and took a full year to learn how tractors are built and marketed. Finally, in 1992 I found a marketing job at Avery Tractors at lower pay. Three years later this company also succumbed to the pressure of mounting imports. My faith in free trade was now shaken. "How many times do I have to retrain to bring food to my family?" I wondered. Senator, each time I called your office to tell my sad story, I was told to join another retraining program. Over the past 30 years, I have been through five such programs, and each time imports killed my new job. Now I have been out of work since 2007, my unemployment benefits have run out, and my family and I live from hand to mouth with my parents. I desperately want another job but just can't find one. All that retraining has offered me little help and no job security. I have no idea what field is left for retraining. So my first question to you, sir, is: Why do you love free trade so much, when it keeps uprooting families like mine?

Senator Caesar: Thank you, Bob, for voting for me over the years. I am sorry to hear that you have had a bad experience with all these imports, costing you one job after another. I became a senator in 1980 and have had many advisers since then; no one has told me imports are bad for our economy. Whenever my constituents complain about cheap foreign goods, how they are made from slave labor and so on, I question my staff, and they always say it doesn't matter why foreign goods are cheap. The fact they are cheap is good for our consumers.

Bob: May I interject?

Senator Caesar: Sure, I am here to listen.

Bob: I have had a lot of time on my hands since 2007. I have a college degree and have been studying our economic history. I found it surprising that all through the 19th century we had very high tariffs, and then the United States became the world's manufacturing leader. My textbook taught me that tariffs kill an economy, so imagine my surprise to discover that American industry was built under an umbrella of tariffs. I still don't believe in them, but can you explain to me why they are bad?

Senator Caesar: Bob, I'm sorry, but this is beyond my expertise; I will ask my adviser to take over. I know I can rely on him completely. AG, can you answer his question?

AG: Sure, it is very simple. Two words—Smoot, Hawley. Have you heard of the Smoot-Hawley tariff? It created the Great Depression. Do we want that again? Of course not!

Bob: I have heard of this argument many times. Please tell me exactly what happened during the Depression.

AG: After the United States sharply raised the tariff rate in 1930 under the Smoot-Hawley legislation, the rest of the world retaliated and passed tariff laws of its own, which ultimately destroyed our export industries. This way our recession became the Great Depression.

Bob: Is it as simple as that?

AG: Yes, it is as simple as that. In fact, you can ask my friend sitting next to me. He is at Harvard and won the Nobel Prize in international economics; he is the Napoleon Bonaparte professor and knows more about this area than anyone else.

NB: Indeed, free trade is my area of expertise, and I believe in it wholeheartedly. Any economist would tell you what the Smoot-Hawley tariff did to our nation and the rest of the world.

Bob: OK, NB, I have been reading history and I found that our GDP fell as much as $47 billion from 1929 to 1933, but our exports were about $7 billion in 1929 and fell to $2.4 billion. Even if all our exports vanished, which they did not, how could our GDP fall by $47 billion from tariffs alone?

NB: Where did you get this information? It is new to me. I have not seen this data.

Bob: I found it in the *Economic Report of the President,* 1984. In fact, I have this little book right here with me. Here, please take a look at pages 220 and 221. It was GNP then and GDP now.

NB: Bob, you have come prepared, haven't you? You sure are digging out something I have never seen or heard before. Let me take a look. OK, 1929 GNP is $103.4 billion, and for 1933 it is $55.8; so it is a fall of . . . well, $47.6 billion. And exports fell by only $4.6 billion. I am puzzled now. Let me think how a 4.6 billion decline can produce a 47 billion decline? Aha! It must be the multiplier effect. You see, there is a formula in Keynesian economics whereby an initial fall in spending causes a magnified fall in demand and hence a large decline in GDP. But to be honest, the multiplier size normally is no larger than three.

Bob: The multiplier does matter, but it also applies to the fall in imports, which, as you can see from page 221, was $3.9 billion. So both our exports and imports dropped, which means the net decline in our exports was only $700 million, and that is nothing compared to the GNP decline. Please don't get me wrong. I have no credentials as an economist, but I keep wondering how a fall of less than a billion in net exports can cause a GNP decline of $47 billion. What do you say, NB?

NB: Bob, you do make a very strong point, and I am going to research it further.

Bob: Doesn't it mean that the entire Smoot-Hawley hoopla tirelessly offered by free traders is a hoax? If GNP declined $47 billion while net exports fell only $700 million, it should be obvious to anyone that the tariff had nothing to do with the Depression. *It is really amazing that no one has cared to look at the facts that are so readily available.*

NB: I concede your point, but tariffs hurt us in many other ways.

Bob: Let me ask you another question: Why are cheap imports good for our consumers, as the senator suggested? Don't they throw people like me out of work? And if we don't have any income, how do prices matter to us? Abraham Lincoln, my hero, once said it is better to produce goods at home, so we have goods as well as our money. What is wrong with this kind of thinking?

NB: Imports do cause job losses, but there are job gains in export industries, so they tend to cancel each other out, and those consumers who retain their jobs benefit from cheap imports.

Bob: That means exports should be as high as imports, otherwise exporting companies will not absorb all those fired in import-competing industries. In other words, we should at least have balanced trade, and not a trade deficit.

NB: Again you make a good point, but sometimes the nation may benefit even with a trade deficit.

Bob: Would you care to give an example?

NB: For example, when imports are so cheap that producing them at home with high wages would be very expensive, and consumers will feel the pain.

Bob: What you are saying is that lower prices are better than higher real wages that come from jobs.

NB: No, I am not saying that. Rather, lower prices generate higher real wages and a higher living standard for all in the long run.

Bob: OK then, imports have soared since the early 1970s, which means real wages should have been rising ever since then. But here I have another book in my briefcase. This one is the *Economic Report of the President,* 2013. Please take a look at this column on page 380. In 1972, real weekly earnings were about $342, but they were only $295 in 2012. What happened to your theory?

NB: I am aware of these figures. But, take a look at page 381 and the figures from 1997 to 2011. You see that the real compensation index rose from 75 to 115. In fact, this index has been growing since 1972, and you will find it in other books. Show me your other report, the one for 1984. Look here, on page 266 it shows a real compensation index of 96 in 1972, compared with 99 in 1983.

Bob: Now I am confused. How can both pages 380 and 381 in the 2013 report be correct? Page 380 reveals a drastic fall in real earnings, whereas page 381 shows a slight rise.

NB: Now I feel wanted. This is why you need economists to explain these things. Page 381 displays figures for all employees in the nation, whereas page 380 offers data only for production workers, and excludes the earnings of supervisors, who, of course, are much richer than the workers.

Bob: Now I get it. These supervisors, I guess, also include CEOs, whose incomes are about 300 times the earnings of production workers. The CEOs and those close to them have benefited excessively from rising imports. No wonder that when you aggregate all incomes, real wages seem to be rising. But that is an illusion because there are very few supervising employees.

NB: You are correct. In fact, production workers are as much as 80 percent of the labor force.

Bob: Then you are undercutting your case for free trade. The policy does not benefit the nation, but only a small segment of the nation at the expense of the vast majority of families: 80 percent have suffered, while 20 percent have benefited from free trade. This is not theory, but reality borne out by history.

NB: That's your opinion, although I now have to agree with you that the case for free trade is not as airtight as I had thought.

Bob: You said earlier that free trade benefits everyone in the long run. From 1972 to 2012, there are 40 years. That is certainly the long run. How come the vast majority of people are still smarting from free trade? You can't deny that 80 percent of the workforce is the vast majority, can you?

NB: Well . . . it does look like the facts are on your side, but free trade has intangible benefits that tariffs don't. Nations are more friendly with each other; international commerce generates peace, while tariffs lead to wars. So I still believe in free trade.

Bob: You make a sweeping statement that cannot be proved. The two world wars of the 20th century occurred in spite of extensive commerce between Germany and its neighbors. Colonies rebelled against England in spite of free trade. It is colonialism that has generated wars, not tariffs.

NB: We can't turn the clock back and resort to tariffs.

Bob: Here I agree with you, but we can at least balance our trade with proper measures. The fact is that I have destroyed your economic case for free trade, but you still love it to preserve international peace, even though it has decimated our middle class. What you are saying is that 80 percent of the workforce should uproot their families because of rising imports, endure repeated bouts of retraining for insecure jobs, so that the other 20 percent may live in luxury and the world does not threaten us with war. I am a lifelong Republican, but if this is free trade, then I want none of it. I have had enough of retraining for a lifetime. Modern economists don't even admit that a nation should export at least as much it imports. This is contrary to the notion of David Ricardo, who invented free trade. I am sorry for raising my voice, but I can't help it. I have suffered for 30 long years so that 20 percent of the nation could trample the economic rights of the other 80 percent. Mr. Goliath, I am done for now. Please yield the floor to Bill, who also has some questions.

David Goliath: Bill, it's your turn now.

Bill: Thank you, David. Bob and I have been friends since 1992, when I was a mechanic for Avery Tractors, and Bob joined us as a salesman. I, too, have been in and out of jobs and moved from one retraining program to another. I have a high school diploma and started work as an auto mechanic in 1975. My first layoff occurred in 1985, when a surge in auto imports forced the shutdown of my company; I retrained myself into tractors and joined Avery the next year. I was laid off, along with Bob, in 1995, and then moved from one lousy job to another for a decade. At least back then I had a job. Since 2007 I have had none. I am over 60 now and am ashamed that my family has to live with my ailing parents, who survive on Social Security and the puny income from their savings. My first question is for Congressman Spartacus.

Congressman, I am a dedicated Democrat and have voted for you ever since 1978. My question is: Why is the Social Security retirement fund empty now when people like me and Bob have paid high taxes for it for more than three decades?

Congressman Spartacus: Thank you, Bill, for voting for me for all these years. Believe me, Bill, I feel very sad that you can't find a job even though the recession ended in 2009. As for Social Security, it is completely safe so long as Democrats are in office. I will never vote to cut the retirement benefits.

Bill: But, Congressman, you did not answer my question. Why is the retirement fund empty? Where has all its money gone?

Congressman Spartacus: It is not completely empty; it has some cash to pay the pensions, and if necessary the administration can borrow money to honor our commitments to retirees.

Bill: Why do you have to borrow to pay pensions when we have already paid high taxes into the fund? I am not a well-read man, but recently my friend Bob gave me a history book to read, and my memory is sharp. I remember being very upset in 1983 when someone proposed raising my payroll tax. I am a Democrat but voted for Reagan in 1980, as he promised to cut my tax bill. By the end of 1983, I learned my Social Security tax would rise for years to come, but the government would put the revenue into a savings account to guarantee my benefits upon retirement. Now you tell me the government may have to take out a loan to pay my parents' pension. Where is that savings account, Congressman? I know my parents live from Social Security check to check, but why should our fund also live like that?

Congressman Spartacus: I know there is barely any money in that fund. But you can't blame me for that. Blame Republican presidents and legislators, including Senator Caesar, who have drained the fund over three decades to award hefty tax cuts to the wealthy.

Bill: It seems both Republicans and Democrats tend to blame each other an awful lot. How did Republicans get away with this? Weren't you supposed to watch out for our interests? I mean, no law can be passed without Democrats getting a chance to vote on it. So how did Republicans manage to loot the fund without your support?

Congressman Spartacus: No, I never supported the looting of the fund.

Bill: But you did vote for their tax cuts.

Congressman Spartacus: Let me think. . . . Yes, I did, and I have regretted it again and again. But now I have vowed they will not touch Social Security benefits if I am elected senator.

Bill: Did you vote for the 1981 tax cut that claimed to fix the budget deficit?

Congressman Spartacus: Yes, I did. I was persuaded by the supply-side rhetoric that trimming the income tax rate would stimulate the economy and balance the budget.

Bill: And then you, along with Republicans, voted to raise taxes in 1982 and 1983?

Congressman Spartacus: Yes.

Bill: What happened to that tax-cut philosophy, Congressman? How in the world could you vote for a tax cut in 1981 to stimulate the economy and then for a massive tax rise in the next two years? No matter what you call it, every tax comes out of someone's income. So you voted to cut the income tax rate and then turned around and replaced that cut with higher taxes in other areas.

Congressman Spartacus: At this point, I don't know why I voted for the tax increase. Had I known the savings account would be looted, I wouldn't have done it.

Bill: May I put the same question to Senator Caesar?

Senator Caesar: I was afraid you would put me on the spot also. Anyway, go ahead with your question.

Bill: We have already established that you cut the income tax rates in 1981 and then raised many other taxes that fall heavily on people with low incomes. Did you not then transfer the tax burden from the rich to the poor? Why do you hate the poor so much?

Senator Caesar: I know, Bill, that you have been without a job for many years and you are angry. But believe me, my votes were not meant to hurt the poor or the middle class. I just wanted to fix the economy the way my economic advisers suggested. I honestly thought we were repairing the battered Social Security system.

Hank Holder: Mr. Goliath, may I join this debate? I know a lot about the history of Social Security, and I am afraid the senator and congressman are not telling the truth.

David Goliath: Wow! The debate is heating up now. PNN is in the business of creating an informed electorate, and today's event, broadcast exclusively by us, indicates my commitment toward widespread public information. Yes, Hank, by all means please join the fray. Why do you think the senator and congressman are not being forthright with us?

Hank Holder: Let me tell you what really happened. It is a long story, but I will be brief. Soon after Reagan was sworn in as president, he proposed a massive tax cut on the incomes of individuals and corporations. Few lawmakers bought his rhetoric that this would balance or even reduce the deficit. But he had won in a landslide, and Democrats were reluctant to oppose his very first piece of legislation. The economy was in bad shape, with huge job losses along with a double-digit rate of inflation. The public was hungry for a new approach, and

the wealthy were sick of paying high taxes. So Reagan got his
tax cuts in mid-1981.

Within weeks of the passage of the new law, some smart-
aleck economists used their calculators and estimated the
budget deficit for 1982, which sent shock waves through
financial markets. For the first time in history, the deficit
estimate crossed not only the $100 billion mark but reached
over $200 billion. Until 1980 the deficit had never surpassed
$75 billion. Interest rates, which were already in double digits
due to giant rates of inflation, shot up further. I remember
hearing about mortgage rates as high as 18 percent. So even
before Reagan's program went into effect, there was a sharp
downturn. Government spending jumped, tax revenue plunged,
and the deficit estimate became a self-fulfilling prophecy.

The only way to bring interest rates down was to
lower the deficit, but that required higher tax rates. So the
lawmakers, including Senator Caesar and Congressman
Spartacus, chose to raise the gasoline tax and payroll taxes.
The public went along willy-nilly, because the administration
guaranteed future pensions and promised to open a savings
account in the retirement trust fund, but the legislators knew
this would never happen. The 1983 Social Security Act
itself authorized the president to use the new revenue in any
way until 1992, and he used it to reduce the federal deficit
rather than put the money in a savings account, which was
not started even after 1992. So the honorable senator and
congressman knew the retirement fund would always be
nearly empty when they voted to raise the payroll taxes. In
fact, they raised taxes only to fund the income tax cut that
they had given mainly to the wealthy and themselves.

David Goliath: Hank, this is a very serious accusation against
these legislators and many others, some of whom are still

serving in the Senate and the House. You mean to say they lie outright whenever they claim they fixed Social Security in the 1980s?

Hank Holder: Indeed, they lie. Since the income tax cut had generated the huge budget deficit in 1982, then they should have raised it back to bring down the deficit. Instead, they chose to raise other taxes to help out wealthy people like themselves, while extracting money from the poor and the middle class. The promised savings account never materialized. Not only that, they repeated their looting of the trust fund in 2001, when they voted to cut income tax rates again. From 1999 on, the trust fund had finally begun to accumulate cash, which was frittered away in 2001 through another cut in income and corporate taxes. I am very angry with what Republicans and Democrats have done to endanger the future of Social Security, and that is why I am a candidate for the Senate. Now I hear that Senator Caesar and the Tea Party want to trim retirement benefits to cut the federal deficit. This is piling outrage upon outrage.

Senator Caesar: We can't change what happened in the past. The reality is that our debt is out of control and we have to do something about it.

Hank Holder: But why do you always pick on Social Security? Is that because the fund is a cash cow, ready to be plundered?

Senator Caesar: I will answer your question with a question. Why do you rob a bank? Because that's where the money is! I am just kidding, but that's what seemed to happen in the past. There was a lot of money coming into the trust fund, so we all, Republicans and Democrats alike, chose to drain it and return its surplus to the people. It is deplorable, and should not be repeated.

Hank Holder: Well, Senator, you returned its surplus mostly to the wealthy, not ordinary people. At least, don't try to cut retirement benefits now and hammer the middle class again. Workers have already paid hefty taxes into the fund, and is it fair to trim their guaranteed pensions from what essentially is their own money? I don't know of any private insurance company that refuses to pay out claims after collecting premiums over several years. Its officers could even go to jail if they committed such a fraud.

Mr. Goliath, may I add a few more remarks?

David Goliath: Yes, by all means.

Hank Holder: I am a historian by training and don't know much about economics; but I do have common sense. It makes no sense to me to ask our hardworking citizens to go through retraining programs again and again whenever cheap imports demolish American jobs. I fully empathize with Bill and Bob; going through one retraining program in your lifetime, I guess, is OK, but going through five is something else. Career politicians fail to understand a person's trauma when he or she is laid off, so they are out of touch with ordinary Americans. When people are fired, their families experience upheaval and uncertainty. By contrast, cushy jobs await politicians even if they lose an election, so they have no idea what losing your livelihood feels like. For example, if I win the Senate election, Mr. Caesar will find a job with one of his patrons without going through any retraining program. There is no reason why our workers repeatedly have to face what career politicians, along with established economists, do not.

[There is hushed silence. . . .]

David Goliath: I think Hank is done. Bill and Bob, do you have any more questions?

Bob: Yes, I do. AG, it is my understanding that the Chicago school is associated with neoclassical economics, of which you, being a Nobel laureate in macro models, are the chief proponent.

AG: I don't know if I am the chief spokesman of this thought, but you are right, many at Chicago are neoclassical economists and believe in the power of free markets.

Bob: Then why do you support oligopolies or monopoly capitalism? According to Adam Smith, known as the father of modern economics, free markets flourish under small firms unable to control wages and prices. But today's giant conglomerates pay low wages and charge high prices. Just look at the prices of gasoline and medicines.

AG: I believe in Adam Smith, but times are different now. We live in a global economy, and we have to compete with the likes of India and China, where wages are low. They, too, have giant firms that can outcompete the best of our companies. So there is plenty of competition, but it is global in nature. In the global context, markets are still free.

Bob: Then you agree that our wages are stagnant because of cheap imports.

AG: I don't believe our wages are stagnant. The economic reports you showed to NB prove that real compensation for all employees has been rising over time.

Bob: These reports also show the real wages have been sinking for 80 percent of the labor force. So how can we possibly say import competition has been good for us? Has it not destroyed the middle class?

AG: My focus is on the nation as a whole.

Bob: You just said that in the global context, our markets are still free. In other words, if there is fierce competition from abroad, it is fine to have oligopolies at home even if they are basically

predators. OK, let me ask you a different question. You
believe that all unemployment is voluntary, right?

AG: Yes, most of it is voluntary.

Bob: In other words, those eight million people who lost their jobs
in 2008 and 2009 left their work voluntarily.

AG: You are trying to provoke me now by putting words in
my mouth. Let me explain why all joblessness is voluntary.
Suppose you are starving; won't you then take any kind of
work to feed yourself? Even if you are a jobless engineer, you
will be ready to work for a company like McDonald's at a tiny
wage. If you don't, then you are jobless by choice.

Bob: That means everyone is jobless by choice and deserves no aid
from the state?

AG: Yes. If you are starving, you should be prepared to work
for the likes of McDonald's, and if you aren't, then you
are voluntarily unemployed and deserve no help from the
government.

Bob: Well said, AG. In 2011, I, a summa cum laude graduate,
tried to find a job at McDonald's, but gave up when I learned
the company had just fired 5,000 workers. My point is that
in a bad economy, during which job losses mainly occur, you
may not be able to find work at any wage. Soon after the
Great Recession, hardly anyone was hiring. If you are right,
then all of those eight million people just quit work, played
games at home, and enjoyed life while subsisting on their
unemployment benefits.

AG: Again, you are putting words in my mouth.

Bob: I also have some questions for NB. Do you believe in this
voluntary unemployment syndrome?

NB: With due respect for my colleague from Chicago, I don't.
Very few people quit their job as wages fall. In fact, almost all
unemployment is involuntary.

Bob: What would you do to fix our economy and restore the lifestyle of the middle class?

NB: I would do more of what the president has done since 2009. I would raise government spending on scientific research, infrastructure, and education. This will increase demand and create more jobs. This will also preserve our status as a technology leader in the world.

Bob: Won't this raise federal debt further? Also, is this not a colossal waste of resources? The president added $8 trillion to our debt by 2014, without raising employment much above the 2007 level. He says things would be lot worse if he had not acted this way. But should we not focus on consumer demand rather than government demand? I mean, come on. Eight trillion dollars in extra debt is about half of our GDP, and all we got for this spending is a nearly constant level of employment. If you divide eight trillion by the number of jobs that have been created, the cost turns out to be several million dollars per job. This sounds like insanity to me. Since the average wage is less than $50,000 per year, we would have been better off just to pay the unemployed to stay at home.

NB: Bob, are you just a college graduate, and not a Ph.D.? You are an expert in presenting facts that a layman can understand. Yes, the debt is enormous and government waste is phenomenal. But what else can we do?

Bob: Have you heard of this new theory of unemployment that has appeared a few times on Truthout.org and is now making the rounds of social media and the Internet? It is called the theory of the wage-productivity gap.

NB: No, I have not. What does it say?

Bob: It says layoffs occur when productivity rises faster than workers' real wage, because rising productivity raises production and stagnant wages create sluggish demand. This causes overproduction and hence layoffs. So the only way to prevent job losses is to adopt policies that close the wage-productivity gap. What do you think of this idea?

NB: Let me think. It sounds like Keynesian economics, where unemployment occurs when supply exceeds demand, but its policy prescription is not the same as raising the government deficit to create jobs.

Bob: That's correct. This theory would rather raise the minimum wage so that the real wage catches up with the enormous productivity rise we have had since 1980.

NB: I also like the idea of raising the minimum wage, but Congress would never go along. What else does the theory recommend?

Bob: The theory also says we should break up the oil companies to bring down gas prices to their free-market level. In fact, the theory suggests we should split all giant firms to bring about free markets to reduce prices, which will then spur consumer demand.

NB: Oh, no way! Even if the idea were to work, Congress would never accept it. Still, the theory is rather intriguing, and I am going to look at Truthout.org.

Bob: You mean our do-nothing Congress would actually do something to stop the move toward free markets? Then we have to find ways to go around Congress and use laws they have already passed.

NB: Good luck with that!

David Goliath: Are you done, Bob?

Bob: Yes, I am. I thank everyone present here.

David Goliath: So do I. This concludes our debate.

PART II

THE CURE

CHAPTER 9

FREE-MARKET OUTCOMES

Banking and Finance

THERE IS LITTLE DOUBT THAT THE FREE ENTERPRISE SYSTEM OF PRODUCtion has proved to be the best economic system ever devised. This is where high GDP growth translates into a rising living standard for all, not just the privileged few. This is where the natural laws of supply and demand work best and society adopts ethical policies. When such laws are flouted, political corruption follows, culminating in unethical measures, high unemployment, and poverty.

History, ancient and modern, offers many examples of how empires collapsed when free enterprise gave way to state enterprise or oligopolies. The Soviet Union is just the most recent example of a system that crumbled under the onslaught of inefficient and unethical decrees.

It was Adam Smith, known as the father of modern economics, who first offered an elegant defense of the theory of free markets, which flourish only when there is keen competition among producers, consumers, and workers. Believing that most people are selfish but rational, Smith assumed that consumers like to buy high-quality goods at the lowest prices, producers seek to maximize profits, and workers want to earn high wages consistent with their hard work and skills. He argued that the material needs and desires of the public are adequately fulfilled only when firms are small and unable to control product prices.

Smith became a celebrated writer when he published his masterpiece, *The Wealth of Nations,* in 1776. Although the Industrial Revolution had started long before his birth, capitalism was still in its infancy. Under the pervasive influence of religion at the time, people were generally suspicious of businessmen's quest for profits and of individualism, which they thought could lead to anarchy. Smith's peers generally championed the interest of the state, not of the masses.

Smith offered a new idea that embraced selfishness as well as people's interest in money and profit. He argued that the pursuit of self-interest and ambition is virtue, not vice, and leads to prosperity, not anarchy. These characteristics motivate employers and employees to put capital and labor to the most productive uses. A firm seeks maximum return from its investment, whereas a worker chases the highest salary for his or her effort. Facing keen competition from others, a producer has to offer high-quality goods at low prices, whereas to compete with their colleagues, employees have to work to their best potential. This is how self-preservation works, at the individual and societal levels.

Businesses, knowing that people want quality products, produce only those goods and services that are in demand, using technology and resources in efficient ways to minimize cost and thus prices. Hence, most people see their needs fulfilled in a free-market economy characterized by intense competition among firms, consumers, and workers. Consumers enjoy superb quality from their low-cost purchases, producers earn adequate profits because they produce goods at minimum cost, and workers enjoy high salaries arising from their hard work. The pursuit of self-interest by everyone thus creates an economy in which society's resources are utilized most efficiently, leading to the highest living standard from available technology. Smith was a champion of small firms to generate keen competition in all industries. He was opposed to all sorts of monopolies or oligopolies among producers or workers.

In terms of actual policy, Smith assailed various government edicts that generated monopolies and restrained business competition. In his view, small-scale enterprises were a constant source of new competitors. These points are noteworthy, because the oligarchs of giant firms tirelessly invoke Smith's vision of free enterprise to defend their outrageous incomes. Rather than denouncing avarice, which is common to us all, Adam Smith denounced government bodies that tolerate mega-mergers by failing to enforce antimonopoly laws, thus restricting competition and in the process generating joblessness and poverty. He justified the profit motive, not profiteering.

Today we don't have free markets; we have monopoly capitalism, and that needs to change. Business practices nowadays annoy customers. As a simple example, suppose you call a company to get some information; the phone may ring five to ten times before you hear a sharp voice: "Hello, for location and office hours, press 1; for directions, press 2; to know what we do, press 3; to talk to our manager, press 4; to talk to the operator and make an appointment, press zero." You press zero, and someone picks up the phone, then puts you on hold for a few minutes, while loud music pierces your ears. If you want to file a complaint against the automated response, there is no button to press. Finally, when the operator turns to you, you seek to talk to customer service. "Please hold," you are told, "the line is busy," and you are left hanging again. You may have to wait for an hour before you talk to the right person. At least, this has been my experience, and most likely yours as well.

Companies know, or should know, that automated responses irritate their customers, but because of the lack of business competition, they no longer care. They just want to minimize cost by minimizing hiring. This way an oligopoly generates minimum jobs, low wages, and dissatisfied consumers.

However, such firms have their defenders, especially among the neoclassical economists. These pundits argue that conglomerates produce goods efficiently by generating economies of scale that lower the cost of production, which eventually benefits consumers. But the vast majority of consumers are also workers, who suffer from merger-induced layoffs or a wage decline. Furthermore, there are also diseconomies of scale, as the merged businesses may become too large for a small group of executives to handle. Many mergers have failed in the past, the most spectacular example being that between America Online (AOL) and Time Warner. In 2002, the year after AOL acquired Time Warner for the hefty sum of $165 billion, the combined company reported a loss of $99 billion, the largest ever suffered by a business.

History shows that many business marriages end in divorce; from what we have seen since the start of the Great Recession in 2007, the current system of monopoly capitalism does not inspire confidence. Should we then break up the industrial giants the way Standard Oil was split into 16 companies in 1911, or the way AT&T was divided into several firms in 1984? My answer is "Of course." Are there any risks to this strategy? After all, breaking up one or two conglomerates is one thing, but splitting many of them is something else.

What could possibly happen? The answer comes from Japan, which was also afflicted by a severe case of monopoly capitalism prior to World War II. Most Japanese industries were vertical monopolies or oligopolies known as *zaibatsu*. (A vertical monopoly includes a holding company that distributes goods to an entire market. AT&T, for instance, was a vertical monopoly until 1984.) Some of them were owned by one family, some by two or three. Sometimes a monopoly had a controlling interest in a bank that financed its operations.

Like their American counterparts today, the *zaibatsu* earned high profits by keeping wages low. They blocked the entry of other entrepreneurs to their markets and treated their workers as virtual serfs. They also had a chokehold on the political system. After the war, the American army occupied Japan. The United States felt that the *zaibatsu* had backed Japanese militarism, so the US Army dissolved the monopolies.

The *zaibatsu* owners were removed from management positions and their company shares sold to the public at discounted prices. Other large firms were also split into smaller units. Eighteen such enterprises, including the well-known Nippon Steel and Mitsui Mining, were so affected. As economist Takafusa Nakamura concludes, "These measures set the stage for the fierce competition which was characteristic of post-war industry in Japan. . . . [T]he plant and equipment expansions and technological advances made under the pressure of competition produced economic growth."[1] This is an understatement, because Japan experienced not just growth but miraculous economic expansion—in a nation devoid of raw materials and sufficient arable land.

Free markets were a great gift from the occupation authorities to Japan, which could not have brought them about on its own. It is very difficult to fight the wealthy interests that dictate politics, even if their actions are perilous for the people. Once the *obanto* (chief executives) of *zaibatsu* lost their privileged positions, business managers were generally hired from the ranks of the younger generation. The young guns were vigorous and visionary. Under their guidance, companies engaged in fierce competition in terms of product quality and technology. All this stimulated innovation and injected dynamism into the economy.

In order to keep costs under control, the companies sharply expanded the subcontracting system that had actually started during the war. This way a firm assigned the production of various parts to subcontractors, which were smaller outfits and paid lower wages.

Prior to the rise of free markets, the giant firms had exploited the subcontractors, paying them very low prices for their output. Now the fierce competition among larger companies made it necessary that new technology be passed onto their parts makers. This is because the quality of final products depends on the quality of parts going into them. In this way, productivity and wages rose not only in major enterprises but also in tiny subcontracting firms. Thus in postwar Japan both large and small corporations flourished. Clearly, the transformation of monopoly capitalism into free markets paid huge dividends to the people, and by 1980 turned Japan into the second-largest economy in the world. Even today, the Japanese economy lags behind only those of the United States and China. Such are the wonders wrought by the transformation of monopoly capitalism into free markets.

THE CASE OF GERMANY

Another nation devastated by World War II was Germany, parts of which were occupied by the US Army. As with the *zaibatsu* system, German industry was also highly monopolistic; furthermore, the German economy was riddled with myriad regulations and price controls. Under pressure from the American army, the nation gradually adopted free-market policies. It lifted price controls on many commodities, introduced currency reforms to replace the old reichsmark with the new deutsche mark, and broke up its two most influential cartels. The iron and steel industry was split into 28 firms, and the chemical giant IG Farben, which gained notoriety during the Holocaust, was broken up into nine companies. These were minor steps toward free-market reforms compared with those in Japan, yet even this little dose of market freedom worked a miracle in the economy.

Europe had been devastated by the war, but German GDP grew at the fastest pace in the 1950s. Its growth rate, 8 percent per year, far surpassed that of its neighbors, such as Britain, France, and Italy. What was unique to Germany, however, was the relative stability of its wage gap in spite of a huge jump in productivity. Our theory says that when productivity grows faster than the real wage, all sorts of distortions emerge quickly in the form of rising debt and poverty, and ultimately rising unemployment. By contrast, *if the real wage outpaces productivity, or is stable despite soaring output per worker, then both joblessness and poverty retreat in a hurry.* That is exactly what transpired in the nation during the 1950s.

Table 9.1 presents data for the wage gap, government debt, and unemployment in Germany from 1950 to 1960. Our theory says if

TABLE 9.1: WAGE GAP, DEBT/GDP RATIO, AND RATE OF
UNEMPLOYMENT IN GERMANY (IN %): 1950–1960

Year	Wage Gap	Debt Ratio	Unemployment Rate
1950	102	19.7	11.0
1951	100	17.5	10.4
1952	106	16.5	9.5
1953	106	21.6	8.4
1954	106	23.1	7.6
1955	107	21.4	5.6
1956	106	19.9	4.4
1957	105	19.1	3.7
1958	106	18.8	3.7
1959	107	18.2	2.6
1960	106	17.4	1.3

Source: Barry Eichengreen and Albrecht Ritschl, "Understanding West German Economic Growth in the 1950s," Working Paper 113/08; US Bureau of Labor Statistics, "International Comparisons of Manufacturing Productivity and Unit Labor Cost Trend," 2011; US Bureau of Labor Statistics, Comparative Civilian Labor Force Statistics, 10 Countries, 1960–2004, 2005.

the wage gap is stable, which it was during that period, the government does not need to raise its debt to preserve jobs. During the 1950s this gap varied within a narrow band of 100 to 106 over 10 years, even though productivity doubled. As a result, the unemployment rate plummeted from 11 percent in 1950 to just 1.3 percent in 1960, even as the federal debt as a percentage of GDP declined from 19.7 percent to 17.4 percent. It should be clear that when the wage gap is stable, the government does not have to overspend to avoid layoffs.

Figure 9.1, in which the wage gap is measured along the left axis and debt and unemployment on the right axis, offers a visual analysis of the events in Germany. What is interesting is that from

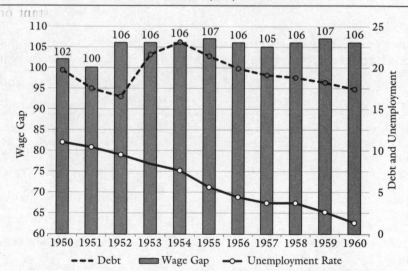

FIGURE 9.1: WAGE GAP, DEBT/GDP RATIO, AND UNEMPLOYMENT RATE IN GERMANY (IN %): 1950–1960

--- Debt   ▬ Wage Gap   ─○─ Unemployment Rate

Source: Barry Eichengreen and Albrecht Ritschl, "Understanding West German Economic Growth in the 1950s," Working Paper 113/08; US Bureau of Labor Statistics, "International Comparisons of Manufacturing Productivity and Unit Labor Cost Trend," 2011; US Bureau of Labor Statistics, Comparative Civilian Labor Force Statistics, 10 Countries, 1960–2004, *2005.*

1952 on the wage gap rose somewhat so that the debt ratio had to increase to bring about a further decline in joblessness. But once the gap stabilized, at around 106, both the debt ratio and unemployment declined steadily.

Next, we examine the German experience during the 1960s, when the economy failed to maintain the torrid pace attained in the previous decade but still enjoyed respectable growth of 4.6 percent per year. The highlight of this decade was an actual decline in the wage gap, something that rarely happens, as the average real wage grew faster than productivity. According to most economists this should have caused high inflation and joblessness, but nothing like this came to pass. The wage-gap index fell from 106 in 1960 to 96 in 1970, whereas the jobless rate declined from 1.3 percent to just 0.5 percent. On the inflation front, Germany's record was so good that the deutsche mark became the most solid currency in the world. A nation that was known for the horrors of hyperinflation became a haven for price stability. Such are the gains from a constant or declining wage gap.

However, price stability was achieved at some cost. With the real wage rising at least as fast as productivity, consumer spending and therefore investment kept up with increasing production, and unemployment at one point dropped to just 0.3 percent of the labor force. Figure 9.2 shows that this occurred in 1964 and 1965. However, for political reasons, government spending jumped at the time, and this, along with high private spending, generated inflation. Bundesbank, Germany's central bank, responded with higher interest rates to control rising prices; demand fell relative to supply, raising joblessness in the process. This is what explains the temporary spike in the unemployment rate in 1966. Soon, however, inflation eased, government spending also fell, and the nation ended the decade with a striking decline in the wage gap and an unemployment rate of 0.5 percent, which was the envy of the entire world.

FIGURE 9.2: WAGE GAP AND UNEMPLOYMENT IN GERMANY: 1960–1970

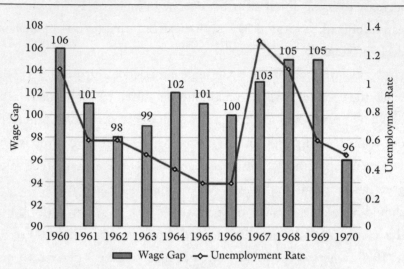

Source: Barry Eichengreen and Albrecht Ritschl, "Understanding West German
Economic Growth in the 1950s," Working Paper 113/08; US Bureau of Labor
Statistics, "International Comparisons of Manufacturing Productivity and Unit
Labor Cost Trend," 2011; US Bureau of Labor Statistics, Comparative Civilian Labor
Force Statistics, 10 Countries, 1960–2004, 2005.

America during the 1950s

While the US government was busy promoting free-market policies
in Germany and Japan, it failed to do so at home. As the economy
shifted from a wartime outfit to peacetime production, the military
technology discovered in the 1940s was utilized in industry. However, this development only increased the growth and dominance of
big business. Most industries—automobile, chemicals, electronics,
tobacco, oil, telephone, computers—became oligopolies, so much so
that just 0.5 percent of corporations came to control 50 percent of
corporate assets.

The labor union movement responded to this consolidation with
consolidation of its own. In 1955 the American Federation of Labor
(AFL) merged with the Congress of Industrial Organizations (CIO)

to form one union, the AFL-CIO. Thus, corporate monopoly power was counterbalanced by union monopoly power. This way, while corporations were able to set prices, they were unable to dictate wages, which were determined through tough negotiations between equally powerful parties. As a result, real wages kept pace with productivity gains arising from advances in technology. In fact, as in Germany during the 1960s, the wage gap declined in America in the 1950s. Such a rare development could not but generate widespread prosperity.

FIGURE 9.3: WAGE GAP AND MEDIAN INCOME IN THE UNITED STATES: 1950-1960*

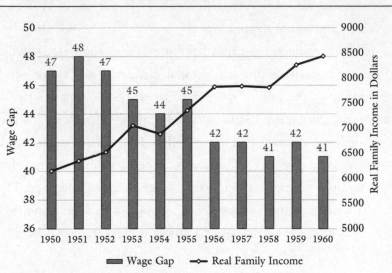

*Median income is also known as real family income.

Source: Council of Economic Advisers, The Economic Report of the President, 1975, p. 274.

First, the unemployment rate fell to as low as 2.9 percent in 1953, a feat never duplicated in US peacetime annals; this happened even though the debt ratio fell, because a lot of wartime debt was being retired every year. However, by 1960 the jobless rate had jumped to 5.5 percent due to a recession induced by rising interest rates.

Second, as displayed in figure 9.3, real family income soared 37 percent during the 1950s, as the wage-gap index fell from 47 in 1950 to 41 in 1960. Interestingly, even though joblessness went up toward the end of the decade, family income continued to climb. Needless to say, poverty fell sharply, as the number of families with annual income below $3,000 plunged 25 percent. This is displayed in figure 9.4. Except in 1954, poverty declined slowly but steadily during the 1950s.

In figure 9.4, the wage gap is on the left axis and the percentage of families below the poverty threshold of $3,000 on the right-hand side. This measure of poverty fell from over 19 percent in 1950 to 13 percent by the end of the decade.

Not surprisingly, the rate of profit fell over the decade, which refutes the hypothesis of tricklism that prosperity seeps down from the wealthy to the poor. Figure 9.5 reveals that except for two or three years, during the 1950s monopoly capitalists suffered a steady profit decline. Meanwhile, poverty fell and prosperity spread to the masses. And remember that all this took place against the backdrop of a marginal tax rate as high as 91 percent on top incomes. Thus the 1950s offer a stinging rebuke to the supply-side dogma and tricklism. They reveal that prosperity actually trickles up, not down.

FREE-MARKET EFFECTS

From the brief discussion of the development experience of the United States, Germany, and Japan, we have learned two precious lessons. First, free markets are best for transforming a destitute and demolished nation into one of lasting prosperity, as was the case with both Germany and Japan following the war. Second, even in the presence of monopoly capitalism, poverty can be lessened if there is a countervailing economic force, such as strong unions, that balances the power of the oligarchs. This was the US experience during

FIGURE 9.4: WAGE GAP AND POVERTY RATE IN THE UNITED STATES (IN %): 1950-1960

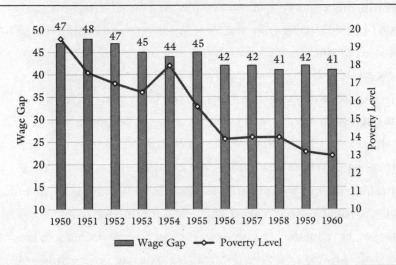

Source: Council of Economic Advisers, The Economic Report of the President, *1975, p. 274.*

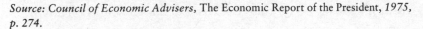

FIGURE 9.5: WAGE GAP AND THE RATE OF PROFIT IN THE UNITED STATES (IN %): 1950-1960

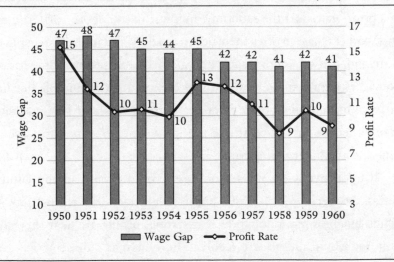

Source: Council of Economic Advisers, The Economic Report of the President, *1975, p. 337.*

the 1950s, as the balancing forces generated an outcome that would prevail only under free-market conditions. Otherwise, how could the rate of profit decline from the lofty levels attained during the 1940s, even as businesses increasingly became oligopolistic; furthermore, how could real wages outpace hefty productivity gains?

Regardless of how you interpret the US experience of the 1950s, the end result was a salutary and widespread decline in poverty. This is the central idea underlying the theory of free-market outcomes. In other words, if politics hinders the creation of competitive capitalism, then create the competitive-capitalism effect in as many industries as possible. Free-market outcomes are inferior to an actual free market, because they require government intervention and a bloated bureaucracy, but given the political reality of an obstructionist Congress, they are far better than tricklism and a voracious oligarchy.

The theory of the competitive-capitalism effect offers a way out of the quicksand that now traps America and the world. My own preference is for market freedom, so that no side of the economic engine is able to abuse its power. Neither firms nor unions should be in a position to hurt the economy. In a free market both corporations and workers have to offer their best to society and in the process generate high growth, high wages, and a reasonable profit. Competition flourishes with competitors, but if there are insurmountable hurdles in breaking up oligopolies to create competitors and free markets, then either we should reinforce the unions or do something else to generate a countervailing force.

It all depends on what Congress would permit in the United States. My feeling is that our legislature prefers the status quo, in which business monopoly power is strong, profits are near their all-time high, and unions are feeble. The oligarchs rule America and have many legislators in their pockets; so the president has to take charge and deliver the poor and the middle class from the damning status quo, where joblessness stays high, poverty continues to rise, and the rich increasingly frolic in luxury with the help of the mushrooming federal debt. The idea is that if free markets are unachievable because of political paralysis, then our commander in chief should step in and generate free-market outcomes. In the lingo of economics, splitting industrial behemoths into smaller firms is a first-best policy, whereas the creation of free-market outcomes is the second-best alternative. However, both measures are vastly superior to the status quo.

The most important sectors in the economy are as follows:

1. Money and banking
2. Retailing
3. Oil and gasoline
4. Pharmaceuticals and health care
5. Foreign trade

We will now show, in this and subsequent chapters, how the president can generate free-market outcomes in all or parts of these sectors without recourse to Congress.

THE FDIC BANK

Let us see how the president, all by himself, can generate a free-market outcome in the area of banking and finance. For the time being, let's ignore foreign trade. Please recall from chapter 5 that in today's America, supply-demand balance occurs when

GDP = Consumer Spending + Consumer Borrowing + Budget
Deficit + Investment

However, total consumer spending, which derives mostly from wages, is hobbled by high interest rates, which also discourage consumer borrowing. In these days of zero percent financing and a near-zero percent federal funds rate, you may find it hard to believe that interest rates are high. Well, they are high where they shouldn't be. They are low in the arena of speculation but enormous in the matter of credit card balances.

The federal funds rate is an interest rate that banks charge each other for overnight loans. It is set by the Federal Reserve and has been at 0.25 percent since December 2008. Needy banks can also borrow money from the Fed at what is called the discount rate, which has stayed at 0.75 percent since early 2010. Both the federal funds rate and the discount rate are near historic lows, which is reminiscent of circumstances during the Great Depression. In December 2007, when the Great Recession is said to have begun, the funds rate was at 4.25 percent, with the discount rate at 5.75 percent. As the financial crisis deepened, the Fed systematically lowered both rates to make more money available to the banks, so they would increase their lending to consumers. The rates were lowered to benefit the public, but that has not happened. Instead the banks made hay by obtaining nearly zero percent financing from the Fed, while charging their noncorporate clients virtually the same rate as before.

Figure 9.6 shows that in November 2007, the average interest rate on credit card balances was around 14 percent, compared with 13 percent in February 2013. In other words, while their borrowing costs plummeted, the banks charged their customers virtually the same rate. Not surprisingly, as seen in figure 9.7, their profit margins on such loans jumped from 6.9 percent to 9.8 percent during the same time period.

Now you see that interest rates are exceptionally high where it matters, because high interest charges on card balances depress consumer spending and borrowing. Meanwhile, the banks pay puny rates on savings accounts and certificates of deposit (CDs). In 2014 you would be lucky to get 1 percent interest on a five-year CD,

FIGURE 9.6: AVERAGE CREDIT CARD INTEREST RATES
(IN %): NOVEMBER 2007–FEBRUARY 2013

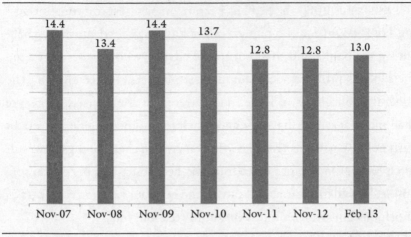

Sources: The Federal Reserve; US Bureau of Labor Statistics; Liana Arnold, CardHub .com.

FIGURE 9.7: AVERAGE CREDIT CARD INTEREST RATE MARGIN
(IN %): NOVEMBER 2007–FEBRUARY 2013

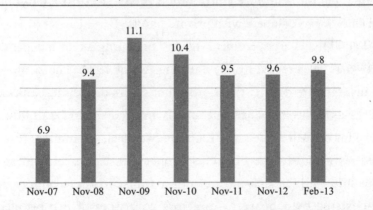

Sources: The Federal Reserve; US Bureau of Labor Statistics; Liana Arnold, CardHub .com.

whereas in 2007 the same CD fetched over 5 percent. No wonder the bankers have pockets full of cash.

Ever since 2007 the Fed has been trying its best to bring borrowing costs down for the public, but it has succeeded mostly in benefiting the banks and their corporate clients, who in turn have used their excess profit to speculate in asset markets—especially oil. The general public, by and large, has suffered in the process. It is true that mortgage rates have plunged, helping homeowners; but credit card holders as well as retirees who survive on their savings have suffered badly. On balance, therefore, the Fed policy has been a failure, and it showed in the anemic state of the economy after seven years of enormous government intervention in free markets.

You may notice that in 2009, when the economy shed 5.5 million jobs, the profit margin of the banks was at its all-time high. How can the government bring interest rates down on credit card loans? The best way would be to break up the big banks and generate competition in the financial industry. Absent that, the president can ask the Federal Deposit Insurance Corporation (FDIC) to start a bank of its own in order to compete with private banks.

The FDIC is a government agency operating as an independent entity that was created by the Banking Act of 1933. The agency offers insurance to protect the money that savers deposit in banks and savings associations. Each account is insured up to $250,000. In return for deposit protection, the agency collects premiums from insured institutions. The FDIC also supervises banks and thrifts to make sure they are solvent and not a threat to the economy. It is administered by a board of directors consisting of five people, of whom three are appointed by the president with the consent of the Senate, and two are ex officio members. One ex officio member is the comptroller of the currency, and the other is the director of the Consumer Financial Protection Bureau. Thus consumer protection is also an important task assigned to the agency.

Even though the FDIC was initially established as a temporary entity, it was soon made permanent, as the government realized its vital importance to the banking system and the economy. In fact, whenever there was a wave of bank failures, Congress expanded its authority to supervise and even take over the failed institutions. The world of banking and finance is particularly prone to fraud, because its managers handle other people's money and are often tempted into making reckless investments to make a quick buck. That is why the FDIC occasionally has been called upon to sort out the mess in our financial system. This happened in the savings and loan crisis in the 1980s and then again soon after the start of the Great Recession.

In case of a failure, the FDIC takes charge of the bank and becomes its receiver. It starts the process of liquidating the bank's nonperforming loans and tries to find another buyer for its deposits and good assets. In most cases, depositors suffer no loss. They usually get a letter in the mail, informing them of their bank's closing, while their account is then held by the new bank. The whole process may be completed over a weekend—from Friday into Monday.

The process is somewhat different if the FDIC is unable to find another healthy bank ready to acquire the failed one. In this case, the agency may start what is known as a bridge bank. In 1987 Congress authorized the agency to establish bridge banks through the Competitive Equality Banking Act (CEBA). The law was designed to enable the FDIC to take over a failed institution and serve its customers without disrupting services.

Over the years the agency has used this power sparingly. During the 1990s it established 32 such banks, usually closing them within two years of their charters. For our purposes, the main point is that the FDIC has the authority to charter its own bank for a maximum of three years through the office of the comptroller of the currency, whose director is an ex officio member of the agency's board of directors. The agency maintains a list of insolvent banks or those close to bankruptcy. It can select one or all of them and pool them into one large bridge bank—hereafter called the FDIC Bank—and then fulfill its other objective of consumer protection in addition to depositor protection. For example, the agency could appoint its own team to replace the current managers and ask it to find a way to bring down credit card rates.

Bank concentration has soared since the 1990s. In 2011, as shown in figure 9.8, just five banks, including JPMorgan Chase, Citigroup, and Bank of America, owned almost half of the industry's assets. As a result, banking profits have soared and their CEOs' incomes have skyrocketed, but all this has come at the expense of their customers, especially credit card holders and small businesses.

FIGURE 9.8: GROWTH OF BANKING CONCENTRATION IN THE UNITED STATES (IN %): 1998–2011

Five-Bank Asset Concentration in the United States

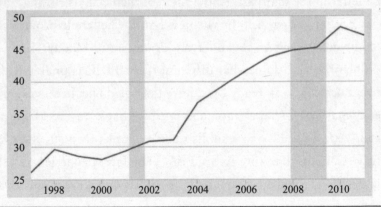

Source: World Bank, 2013; Federal Reserve Bank of St. Louis, 2013.

The agency is empowered to lend money to a bridge bank from its own funds. This way the FDIC Bank could be properly capitalized, which would enable it to borrow money from the Federal Reserve at a bare minimum rate of 0.75 percent, just like other healthy banks. In 2014 the agency had more than $40 billion in its deposit insurance fund; it is also authorized to borrow up to $100 billion from the Treasury.

Once the agency's bank is fully capitalized and operational, it could invite credit card owners to transfer their loan balances to the FDIC Bank, and charge them a low rate of 5 percent. Presto, the card rates would plunge, because then the other large banks would have to compete with the bridge bank or lose a substantial number of card holders. The boost that this move would give to the economy is hard to fathom.

In 2014 credit card debt approximated $854 billion, on which the average interest rate was 13 percent. If this rate dropped to 5 percent, card holders would save $68 billion in interest fees. Furthermore, the saving would accrue to them every year and would work like a hefty tax cut. This measure alone would raise consumer spending sharply. The establishment of the FDIC Bank would result in a free market in the arena of finance, inconvenience the large banks that have been preying upon the destitute, and in the process reduce speculation in the oil market.

In October 2014, the Fed terminated its multiple schemes of bailing out Wall Street and financial firms by ending what is call quantitative easing. It took only two months for the oil price to fall drastically, but the price was still above its free-market value. Now you see how much harm the Fed had done by intervening in free markets and brazenly supporting the speculators, who had kept the petrol price sky-high in the midst of plummeting US demand for oil. Once the FDIC aims to generate competition in the banking industry, it could provide a strong antidote for other forms of financial mismanagement and interventions by the Federal Reserve. Moreover, Congress would be unable to obstruct the return of prosperity, because the law authorizing the FDIC to capitalize its own bank already exists.

Now the question is: Can a bank remain profitable with an interest rate margin on credit card balances barely above 4 percent? If the

FDIC Bank charges 5 percent, while it pays 0.75 percent to the Fed for loans or less than that on CDs or savings accounts, then its profit margin will be much lower than that of other banks. Can the bridge bank survive on a relatively small margin? It certainly can, and the proof comes from the historical data on credit card rates. Figure 9.7 shows that in November 2009, when the economy had already lost eight million jobs over two years, the banks' profit margin on card balances, at 11 percent, was the highest in recorded data. In other words, bankers were the most ruthless when the newly unemployed were the most helpless and the nation was in despair. Millions of families presumably lived partly on credit cards to survive. With those newly jobless in shock, the banking industry squeezed them at the maximum rate—because it could get away with it. With little competition in the industry, the large banks copied each other and charged nearly the same rates from their clients.

However, the interest margins were not always this high. Figure 9.9 reveals a relatively benign face of the banking structure. In

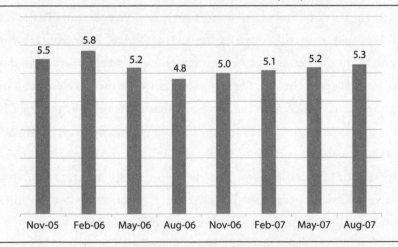

FIGURE 9.9: CREDIT CARD INTEREST RATE MARGINS (IN %): 2005–2007

Sources: Federal Reserve; US Bureau of Labor Statistics; Liana Arnold, CardHub .com.

August 2006, about a year prior to the start of the recession, the interest margin was a lowly 4.8 percent. If the big banks that offer multimillion-dollar pay packages to their executives could be profitable on a 4.8 percent margin, then the FDIC Bank, with its government-appointed managers working for a fraction of what other banks pay, would certainly be able to make money on a similar profit margin. In 2006, according to the Federal Reserve, the financial industry earned $414 billion in spite of its huge administrative costs, which shows that the FDIC Bank, because of its lower cost structure, would be very profitable.

AID FOR SMALL BUSINESS

There is no reason why the bridge bank should limit its activity to the transfer of credit balances. It can also issue its own cards, such as MasterCard and Visa, and lower the commission that banks normally charge retailers. At present, a merchant typically pays a 2 percent fee on a purchase involving these cards. On a transaction of $100, the retailer pays a commission of $2, of which $1.50 goes to the issuing bank and the other 50 cents go to various intermediaries engaged in servicing and processing the transaction. If the FDIC Bank issues its own cards and reduces its charge to 75 cents, then every merchant will gain that much on a $100 transaction. This will help the currently beleaguered small-business person. The merchant will now end up with $98.75 instead of $98. This is another way the FDIC Bank could assist the poor and the middle class. It would be especially beneficial to the self-employed, who bear the maximum burden of the current tax system.

Major banks sting their customers in many other ways. As business writer Meagan Clark reported in September 2014, "The average fee for using an out-of-network ATM has risen 5 percent over the past year and 23 percent over the past five years, while the average overdraft fee has risen for the 16th consecutive year."[2] The FDIC Bank can also compete with financial giants in these areas and bring those hefty fees down to the free-market levels that prevailed at the start of the new millennium. With banking behemoths squeezing the public left and right, it is clear that the FDIC Bank would perform an invaluable service for the nation.

RETIREE BONDS

Epic intervention by the Federal Reserve in the savings markets since 2007 has been catastrophic for retirees. Even the Fed realizes the vital importance of consumer spending for growth and employment. Yet its actions in this regard have been counterproductive. Nearly zero percent interest rates are designed to revive business and residential investment, but even in the best of times investment in the United States is below 20 percent of GDP, whereas consumer spending is usually above 66 percent. Is it then prudent to overemphasize investment at the expense of consumption?

Is the Fed simply misguided? Yes. Its actions reflect the pervasive influence of oligarchs and tricklism, whereby official policies give priority to pro-business measures. The Fed assumes that low interest rates spur business investment and thus create jobs. However, consumer spending, not borrowing cost, is the most effective stimulus to investment. Think about it. If you can't sell all that you can produce, would you expand your business even if the interest rate falls to zero? Business expansion in the face of sluggish demand would only increase your risk of loss. Low interest rates do spur residential investment, but not in the middle of a recession.

However, the Fed is not likely to alter its policy for a long time, which means the president must create a free-market outcome in the savings market as well. The Treasury can issue five-year bonds, paying the interest rate available on a regular 30-year bond sold in auctions (an average of 3.5 percent in 2014) and make them available only to needy retirees. A pensioner with an annual income no larger than $50,000 should qualify to buy the five-year option. In 2014 the interest rate on a five-year CD averaged less than 1.5 percent; so long as the market CD rate is below the 30-year bond rate, needy retirees would keep renewing their five-year bonds. This way their interest income would rise, but the Treasury would see little increase in its borrowing cost.

For example, suppose you buy a five-year bond from the Treasury at a simple interest rate of 3.5 percent. If you invest $100, you will earn $3.50 per year instead of $1.50, and if you renew your bond every five years at the same rate, then for the Treasury it will become a 30-year bond. Thus, the government's borrowing cost will not change. If the retiree passes away prematurely, then the Treasury will buy the bond back for $100. The government's cost of borrowing would climb only if the interest rate rose above 3.5 percent, which would indicate that the economy had become normal. This would be a highly desirable outcome at very little cost to the government.

While the government's borrowing costs would not likely increase through the retiree bond scheme, the boost to the economy would be strong and immediate. First, needy pensioners would escape poverty to some extent; second, consumer spending would rise; and finally, with other interest rates remaining low, the creation of retiree bonds would generate additional benefits for the economy. The policy of competitive capitalism in the arena of banking and finance would thus give an immediate and indispensable boost to our fragile system.

CHAPTER 10

FREE-MARKET OUTCOMES

Oil and Gasoline

IN 1998, WITH THE UNITED STATES STRONG AND HEALTHY BUT THE REST OF the world in a slump caused by the ongoing Asian currency crisis, the international price of oil averaged a lowly $11.90 per barrel. Regular gasoline in California, a state notorious for expensive gas, ended the year at $1.13 per gallon. Barely 10 years later, in July 2008, the petrol price surpassed the lofty level of $147 per barrel, while California's per-gallon gas cost peaked at $4.58. What could have transpired in just a decade that raised the international oil cost by more than 1,100 percent, stinging America's drivers and economy at the same time? Once again: monopoly capitalism, or oligopolies in the oil market.

It is rightly said that oil is the lifeblood of modern economies. Energy plays a vital role in virtually every industry, so that its price significantly affects global economic performance. In factories, machines need energy to run. Homes need it for cooling, heating, and lighting. An oil-price hike afflicts an economy in myriad ways. First, operating cost rises for producers, who then have to trim their output. Second, since America imports more than half of its required amount of oil, an increase in energy prices raises those imports and enhances the trade deficit, which is a major drain on the nation's GDP. Third, consumers use gasoline for commuting, airlines use it to fly airplanes, and trucks need it to transport goods across the nation, and expensive oil hurts them all. Thus, both consumers and producers are vulnerable to petrol-price hikes.

Why should the supply of a product decline because of a rise in the cost of production? A simple example illustrates the point. Suppose you have a business that builds chairs and have $100 for investment. If the average production cost is $5, you can build 20 chairs with your capital; if the cost doubles, then you can make only 10 chairs. Thus supply falls with a rise in average production cost.

In economics the twin concepts of supply and demand explain almost all activity, which suggests that price bubbles can form in two ways. Either demand for something regularly runs ahead of supply, or supply is so constricted that it constantly falls short of demand. Hence there are two types of bubbles—demand driven and supply driven. When the supply of a product declines relative to its demand, its price normally rises, while its output goes down. This is exactly what happened to petroleum in the 1970s and again in the early 1980s. During the 1970s oil prices rose frequently as OPEC restrained its output below the level of global demand. As a result, the petrol price kept rising to reduce demand to the level of production. Thus the petroleum bubble of the 1970s was chiefly a supply-oriented bubble.

However, bubbles are usually vulnerable to recessions, as you can see from figure 10.1. The petro-bubble began in 1973, when OPEC first imposed an oil embargo and later jacked up the price by controlling its output. The 1970s witnessed periodic shortages of oil that occasionally resulted in long gas lines. I remember once sitting in my car for an hour before I could get near a pumping station to replenish my tank with the maximum-allowed 10 gallons of gasoline. There have been no gas lines in recent years, yet some experts claimed there was a shortage of oil around the world after 2009, which justified its triple-digit price.

FIGURE 10.1: AVERAGE ANNUAL CRUDE PRICES IN
THE UNITED STATES ($/BARREL): 1973–1986

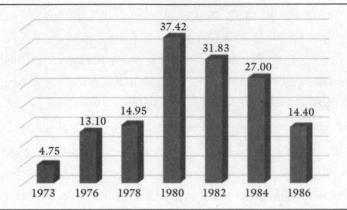

Source: Tim McMahon, "Oil Prices 1946–Present," inflationdata.com.

Another disruption in oil supply occurred during the revolution in Iran in 1979, and the petrol price rocketed again. However, despite such powerful forces working to cut the output, the petro-bubble popped after 1982. The average oil price jumped from $4.75 in 1973 to over $13 in 1976, peaking in 1980 at $37.42; thereafter it began to fall, at first slowly and then in a hurry. The sharp recession in the United States and around the world had something to do with it. By 1986 the oil price had collapsed to just $14. In other words, once the recession hit the world, two large disruptions in oil output were unable to sustain its hefty price.

Now let's look at the oil bubble that started in 2000. We know from figure 5.5 in chapter 5 that the petrol price collapsed again in

1998 but recovered by the end of the decade and began a slow but steady climb. An oil bubble always forms a gasoline bubble, because the two are intricately related. This time we examine the behavior of gas prices in the state of California, which is said to have the seventh- or eighth-largest economy in the world, and is also notorious for expensive energy prices. As seen in figure 10.2, regular gasoline averaged around $1.65 in December 2000, began a slow climb thereafter and peaked around $4.55 in July 2008, the month when the international oil price peaked at $147. Then the bubble popped and gasoline ended at $1.81 by year's end.

However, the pop was only temporary, because the Bush administration and the Federal Reserve bailed out the army of speculators. Unlike in 1982 and subsequently in 1998, the petrol price collapse lasted only a few months, even though the globe experienced the worst recession since the Great Depression. Figure 10.3 reveals something extraordinary. The oil and gas bubble resumed in 2009, while millions were still being laid off. By June 2014, California's regular gas had again surpassed $4 per gallon. Thus, when our government and the Fed are in cahoots with OPEC and oil oligarchs, even a mega-recession cannot suppress the oil bubble.

The oil-price hike is like a big tax increase on both consumers and producers. As explained above, it raises the cost of consumption or production for almost everyone in the economy. The only beneficiaries are the oil barons around the globe. How did the apologists for cartels explain the ongoing petro-bubble?

They usually advanced three arguments to justify the oil spike in a milieu of low demand for crude in the United States:

1. Peak oil
2. Terrorism risk or uncertainty in the Middle East
3. Blistering rise in oil demand from India and China

FIGURE 10.2: AVERAGE WEEKLY GASOLINE PRICE IN CALIFORNIA ($/GALLON): DECEMBER 1998–DECEMBER 2008

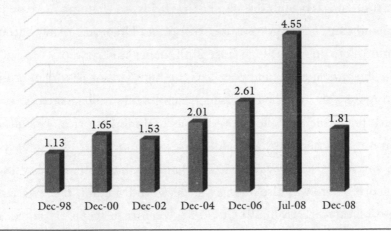

Source: Energy Information Administration, California Energy Consumption, © State of California, energyalmanac.ca.gov.

FIGURE 10.3: AVERAGE WEEKLY GASOLINE PRICE IN CALIFORNIA ($/GALLON): DECEMBER 2008–JUNE 2014

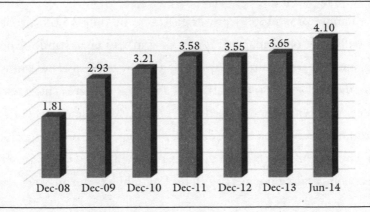

Source: Energy Information Administration, California Energy Consumption, © State of California, energyalmanac.ca.gov.

The first argument states that oil output has peaked around the world either because of soaring drilling costs or because of the exhaustion of a large number of existing fields, so that any increase in demand causes a large rise in petrol price. However, rising output from American fields alone since 2000 belies this view.

The second argument concerns the high risk of terrorism originating from the Middle East, which enables oil producers to demand a risk premium over and above the normal market price. The question is this: When was the Middle East not in turmoil? Ever since the six-day Arab-Israeli War in 1973, that area has suffered relentless violence. There was also a long war between Iran and Iraq, two major oil producers, from 1981 to 1988. Terrorism seems trivial compared with actual war. If this eight-year war could not prevent the oil price collapse in 1986, why should terrorism stop it? The risk premium from a long war is much higher than that from terrorism. The point is that uncertainty about oil supply from the Middle East is always present, and it could not keep the petrol price from plunging whenever the world was hit by even a minor recession. Thus, the huge oil-price jump between 2000 and 2014 was mostly the result of the vast abuse of monopoly power exercised by the two oil cartels.

Finally, the oil demand from India and China has indeed been rising, but that from Europe, America, and Brazil has been declining. Furthermore, if supply rises just as fast as demand, there is little rise in product price. And supply indeed has kept pace with demand. Thus all the arguments advanced by the defenders of expensive oil are specious. Then why was oil not cheap in the midst of anemic economic growth? The economist and oil expert William Engdahl has the answer:

> The oil price today, unlike twenty years ago, is determined behind closed doors in the trading rooms of giant financial institutions like Goldman Sachs, Morgan Stanley, JP Morgan Chase, Citigroup, Deutsche Bank or UBS.[1]

You may have noticed that these are also among the institutions that received the lion's share of the Bush bailout and aid from the Fed. Some of them also benefited from the money received from the European Central Bank. They and a few others are the principal players in oil speculation. However, there would be little speculation if these players were unsure about the ability of oil cartels to control prices. Remember that OPEC alone was unable to sustain the petrol price in the 1980s and the late 1990s. Something happened beginning in 1998 that greatly magnified the oil industry's monopoly power. By then there had been 2,600 mergers in the industry, but they mostly involved small firms. So the petrol market was not fully oligopolistic yet. By 2001, however, there were mega-mergers that completely transformed the face of the industry:

1. BP acquired Amoco and ARCO.
2. Exxon merged with Mobil to form ExxonMobil.
3. Total acquired Petrofina and Elf Aquitaine to form Total SA.
4. Chevron acquired Texaco.
5. Conoco merged with Phillips Petroleum, forming ConocoPhillips.

Thus 12 major companies became five, and their control over the petrol price magnified. Add to this the government's direct assistance in the form of bailouts to speculators in Europe and North America, and the oil industry has now become the biggest predator in the world. Even huge declines in gasoline demand from the world's largest consumer, the United States, could not subdue the beast.

Please examine two graphs from the 2014 *Economic Report of the President (ERP)*. Figure 10.4, which is a reproduction of figure 2–18 from the *ERP*, displays a relentless drop in US net oil imports since 2005. As the *ERP* describes it:

In 2013, the United States continued to benefit from developments in the oil and gas sectors, as well as from growth in energy efficiency and the production and integration of renewable energy. As shown in Figure 2–18, net petroleum imports have fallen from more than 12 million barrels a day in 2005 to approximately 6.2 million barrels a day in 2013. Moreover, as shown in Figure 2–19, beginning in October 2013, domestic crude oil production exceeded crude oil imports for the first time since 1995.[2]

This passage from the *ERP* makes it clear that there has been a sharp drop in American petrol imports since 1995. In fact, by 2013 such imports were cut in half, or by about six million barrels per day. Then why was the oil price so high that year? The *ERP* graph also shows that from 1980 to 1985, daily oil imports fell by about two million barrels, and we know that in 1986 the oil price plunged to a mere $14. Thus in 1986 a puny drop in American demand caused an oil collapse, whereas in 2013, oil kept rising in spite of a much bigger fall in demand. Something has clearly changed for the worse, but the *ERP* writers are not interested in finding out.

In fact, the administration's economists offer another graph, reproduced here as figure 10.5, that reveals vast inconsistencies in their approach to economic policy. This graph shows a major decline in America's daily use of gasoline since 2000; yet the retail gas price had risen from about $1.50 per gallon in 2000 to over $3 by 2013.

THE FREE-MARKET OUTCOME IN OIL

What can we do to bring oil to its knees, where it belongs in an anemic economy? The free-market petrol price in 2014 was no higher than $20 per barrel. Figure 10.4 shows that American oil imports that year approximated their 1987 level, when oil averaged around

FIGURE 10.4: PETROLEUM NET IMPORTS (MILLION BARRELS PER DAY): 1980–2015

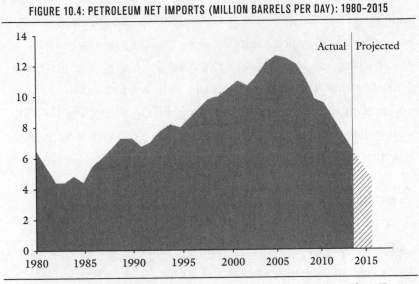

Source: Energy Information Administration, Monthly Energy Review, "Short-Term Energy Outlook."

FIGURE 10.5: US PER-CAPITA CONSUMPTION OF GASOLINE
AND REAL GASOLINE PRICES, 2000–2013

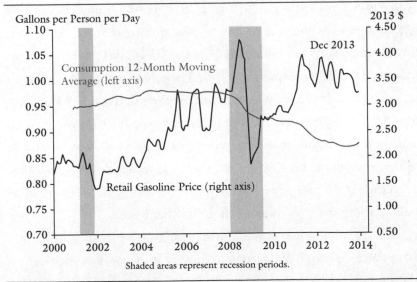

Shaded areas represent recession periods.

Source: Energy Information Administration, Monthly Energy Review; Census Bureau; Council of Economic Advisers calculations.

$18 per barrel in spite of a furious ongoing war between Iran and Iraq. That is about where the petrol price should have been in 2014, given that US oil imports were more or less the same as before.

The simplest way to lower the price is to raise the margin requirements for oil speculation. This margin is regulated by the Commodity Futures Trading Commission (CFTC), which like the FDIC is an independent agency, but is part of the executive branch of the government. The CFTC website defines its mission as follows:

> The mission of the Commodity Futures Trading Commission (CFTC) is to protect market participants and the public from fraud, manipulation, abusive practices and systemic risk related to derivatives—both futures and swaps—and to foster transparent, open, competitive and financially sound markets.[3]

Please note that CFTC's mission in a nutshell is to prevent fraud and generate competitive markets. With OPEC along with five or six oil conglomerates dominating the market, and with petrol prices at or near triple digits between 2010 and 2014, the oil industry is clearly not competitive, and indeed has been committing fraud. However, this fraud could be eliminated if only the CFTC were to treat oil futures as it would a company's shares. The margin requirement for oil futures is just 6 percent, whereas for company shares it is 50 percent. In other words, if you want to buy a stock worth $100, you have to make a down payment of $50, whereas to buy $100 worth of oil to be delivered in the near future, all you have to put down is $6. With a leverage of 16 to 1, there is much greater scope for speculation as well as abuse in the oil market than in other assets.

The question is why should futures markets be treated differently from share markets? We learned to our great sorrow how stock speculation in the 1920s generated a disastrous depression in the 1930s; in order to counter such threats, the government subsequently raised the minimum down payment for the purchase of company shares. Are we going to wait for a similar calamity before we do something about oil speculation? I hope not.

Does the CFTC have the authority to increase the margin requirement? According to energy specialist David Sheppard, "The CFTC already has emergency powers to raise margins, though they have rarely exercised them."[4] Bahattin Buyuksahin, a research adviser to the Bank of Canada and a former econometrician at the CFTC, also confirms that the futures agency has this authority.[5] Clearly if the agency is allowed to regulate margins, it can boost them as well.

Do we have an emergency in the oil market? Yes, indeed. The oil oligarchs are not only manipulating the futures markets; their actions are also fraudulent. The 2014 *ERP* report reveals that there has been a relentless decline in US oil imports ever since 2005. We now import less crude than in 1995, some 20 years ago. If markets were competitive, there would have been a drastic fall in the international price of oil, as happened in 1986 and 1998. This is what happens to necessities, which in the lingo of economics have inelastic demand. Economics 101 teaches us that even a slight fall in the demand for necessary or inelastic goods such as oil and gasoline leads to a very large decline in their price. And oil and gasoline are certainly necessary goods indispensable to modern economies.

However, oil remained sky-high in spite of a ten-year fall in American imports. If this is not price gouging, what is? This is clear-cut evidence of fraud and manipulation in the global oil market, and it suggests that the CFTC ought to use its emergency powers to fulfill its mission, which is to ensure competition in the industry and eliminate chicanery.

Suppose the CFTC were to raise the down payment for buying an oil-futures contract to 50 percent. What could possibly happen? Big banks, hedge funds, and other speculators would have to borrow more money or use their own cash to engage in oil trading, which, because of increased borrowing costs, will immediately plunge. So will the artificial demand for oil. The petrol price will plummet overnight.

What about the refineries, which genuinely need crude to turn it into gasoline? Will they be hurt in any way? Their cost could also climb because of increased margins, but they rarely engage in speculation; in any case, the benefit from a substantial decline in the price of their raw material will far outweigh any cost increase. It is hard to imagine that enhanced margins for oil futures could harm anyone but the oil oligarchs; however, the boost to the global economy will be vast enough to be incalculable.

There is also some evidence of how increased margins trimmed crude prices in the past. According to Ray, another energy specialist, "Historically, when margins are raised, oil prices fall. This is exactly what happened in February 2011. Oil prices dropped 10 percent in a few months. A year later these margins were lowered, and oil prices spiked back up to 109 dollars a barrel."[6] These were minor changes in margins and still generated noteworthy changes in crude prices. If margins were raised substantially, clearly the crude price would plummet to the free-market level, which, as argued above, is no higher than $20 per barrel. Thus, the president can bring the oil price down by simply persuading the CFTC to take bold action, without having to go through Congress. The CFTC already has the needed authority to do this and does not require any new power.

Figure 10.2 reveals that in December 1998, California's gasoline price was $1.13. That is where this price should be today, because US oil imports have dropped sharply since then. However, it all depends on the CFTC.

CHAPTER 11

FREE-MARKET OUTCOMES

Big Pharma and Foreign Trade

WHEN COLUMBUS SAILED IN UNCHARTED WATERS, HE WANTED TO DISCOVER an alternate sea route to India; he discovered America instead, and soon was born the legend of the American dream. He and his cohorts brought home gold, silver, and tales of an amazing land, mostly uninhabited and free from oppression. Soon all of Europe knew about the promise of the new continent, and tens of thousands left their homes to start life afresh, in a world where they could live in freedom, escape poverty, and pursue the religion of their choice. Such was the vision of the Pilgrims and others who settled in areas along the northeastern border of what today is the United States.

Britain, Spain, and France vied for the control of North America, but the British won out in their quest for colonies. It made great business sense to Britain to be the uncontested master of the new world, which could provide it with much-needed raw materials in exchange for industrial goods. Not surprisingly, an English businessman, David Ricardo, developed a theory to suggest that the American colonies should focus on the production and export of farm goods and minerals and obtain manufactured products from England. So long as this bilateral trade was in rough balance, he argued, both sides would prosper, and any restraint on commerce in the form of tariffs would hurt them both. Thus was born the theory of free trade, which has been gospel among economists for a long time.

Now there is a wide variety of taxes, such as levies on wages, profits, sales, self-employment, and so on, and we harried taxpayers know all about them. However, Ricardo argued that tariffs were something special and should be avoided at all costs. Other types of taxes were fine, but levies on imports were self-destructive. If you are cynical and sensible, you can easily see through the self-serving motive behind Ricardo's sweeping assertion that the exchange of goods alone with another country raises a nation's living standard. To him there was no need for the colonies to industrialize, as Britain could fill their needs for manufactured goods. This way Ricardo's business mind sought to ensure lasting prosperity for British industry, which could not only obtain inexpensive raw materials but also retain captive markets for its goods.

America ceased to be a British colony in 1776 and became an independent republic in 1789, but the legend of the American dream has remained alive to this day. In fact, the concept became a global dream. Following the birth of the Republic, people from all over the world sought to come to the United States.

When I finished my MA degree from the Delhi School of Economics in 1965, with an A, my first thought was that I could now qualify for a scholarship and go to America to earn a PhD. To me the United States appeared as the land not only of riches but also of justice, liberty, and honesty. After I arrived here, in 1966, my expectations were more than fulfilled. One morning I saw a student leave a stack of newspapers at the doorstep of the campus library, in which I occasionally used to sit and study for a few hours; then professors and some other students came, each picking up a paper and placing a dime in a metal box that the entrepreneurial boy had left behind. I had never seen such honesty before. No one took the newspaper for free. A few hours later the paper boy came back, collected the money, and left. That was how he partly supported his studies.

Over the years, I have seen a gradual erosion of such honesty, but even now Americans in general are hardworking, decent, and helpful to those in need. Crime has indeed spread, but mostly because of the insatiable greed of the oligarchs and their hirelings. When leaders become corrupt, their virus is bound to infect the general public. Still, this infection is not so widespread, especially compared with what has happened in many other nations, where corruption has become a way of life.

Since its independence, the United States has seen vast ups and downs in terms of poverty and prosperity, yet the ethos of the American dream has endured. At the same time, the oracle of free trade, that relic of the colonial past, has also survived—has, in fact, continued to find many followers among economists. Never mind that American pioneers rejected Ricardo's argument and built the nation's industry with the help of high tariffs.

The lure of the American dream lived through the Great Depression. In fact, James Adams wrote his masterpiece, *The Epic of America*, in 1931 in the midst of darkening gloom and gave a broader meaning to the concept, stating that Americans live in

a land in which life should be better and richer and fuller for everyone, with opportunity for each according to ability or achievement. It is a difficult dream for the European upper classes to interpret adequately, and too many of us ourselves have grown weary and mistrustful of it. It is not a dream of motor cars and high wages merely, but a dream of social order in which each man and each woman shall be able to attain to the fullest stature of which they are innately capable, and be recognized by others for what they are, regardless of the fortuitous circumstances of birth or position.[1]

However, as prosperity returned following World War II, the American dream again acquired a more materialistic ethos. In 1992 Michael Wolff et al. wrote that the dream means "a home of your own, money in the bank, a big car, appliances galore, all provided by a single wage earner."[2] In recent years these requirements have changed somewhat, as single-earner families have been largely replaced by two-earner households, who need two cars to commute and also want iPhones, personal computers, and flat-screen TVs.

Unfortunately, today, as in the 1930s, the American dream seems elusive to much of the public. A poll conducted in 2013 found that 41 percent of the people were pessimistic about their future while only 38 percent were optimistic.[3] For us the big question is: What built the American dream, and what is slowly killing it? Is it free trade that erected the vast industrial colossus? Of course not!

The Ricardian theory says a nation should specialize in export industries and fulfill other needs with imports. At its birth, the United States was overwhelmingly a farm economy. So if early American presidents had adhered to this theory, today we would be known around the world as a first-rate agrarian nation. We would have little industry and meet our needs for manufactures mostly by obtaining them from overseas. Without industrialization no American would have set foot on the moon, nor would our nation have defeated Hitler in the war. Then how did we build our economy and become the mightiest economic power on Earth? Let us take a look at our history.

In 1800, according to figure 11.1, barely 5 percent of the labor force worked in manufacturing; 70 percent worked in agriculture and 20 percent in assorted services. The remaining 5 percent was employed in other occupations, such as government service, the army, and so on. The tax system was very simple.

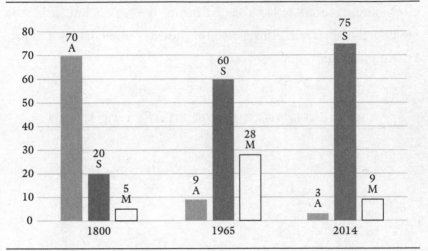

FIGURE 11.1: PERCENTAGE OF LABOR EMPLOYED IN AGRICULTURE (A),
SERVICES (S), AND MANUFACTURING (M) IN THE UNITED STATES: 1800–2014

Source: Gilbert Fite and Jim Reese, An Economic History of the United States (Boston: Houghton Mifflin, 1973); Council of Economic Advisers, The Economic Report of the President, 2014.

There was no income tax and no sales tax on goods; tariffs were also low, ranging from 5 to 15 percent. The United States exported corn, wheat, and cotton in return for textiles, machinery, and crude appliances from abroad. Then something occurred in 1812 that would change the course of American history. In retrospect it was a fortuitous development: England declared war against its former colony. Manufactured imports vanished, their prices rose sharply, and the United States was forced to develop its own industry, especially in cotton textiles, whose production rose from 648,000 yards in 1810 to over 2.3 million yards in 1815, the year when the war ended. At that point the British dumped their goods to regain their lucrative market, and in 1816 US output plunged to 840,000 yards. The resulting hue and cry from domestic producers induced Congress to more than double the tariff rates to a range of 15 to 30 percent. The rest is history. This was the start of a long process of industrialization, and for this the credit goes solely to the Tariff Act of 1816. First, see how surging imports wasted the American economy in 1816, as cloth output shrank to less than half from the year before, and then see how the new tariff rejuvenated the industry immediately and preserved jobs and wages.

FIGURE 11.2: GROWTH OF COTTON TEXTILES IN NEW ENGLAND: 1810–1860

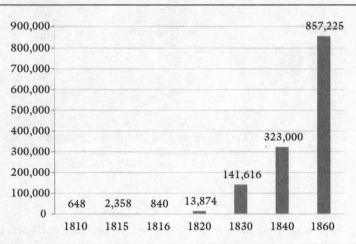

Source: Robert Zevin, "The Growth of Cotton Textile Production After 1815," in Robert Fogel and Stanly Engerman (editors), The Reinterpretation of American Economic History (New York: Harper & Row, 1971), table 1, pp. 123–24. (The pre-tariff textile output is so low that it does not even show up in the graph.)

Figure 11.2 displays the real story of the textile industry. By 1860 its output had rocketed to over 800 million yards of clothing. How could this tariff possibly hurt the nation? Furthermore, how did the country achieve such a monumental jump in this output? It followed a formula that was later emulated by many other nations after World War II, such as Japan, China, South Korea, Taiwan, and Singapore, among others. America imported machinery and technology from Europe and employed them to transform its own production of raw cotton and wool into cotton and woolen textiles, while its tariffs restrained imports and enabled local producers to pay wages much higher than those in Britain. Note that higher American wages did not keep the nation from the torrid pace of industrialization; in fact, they raised its living standard above that in Europe and attracted swarms of immigrants. Foreign investment also surged.

Labor moved from farming into manufacturing. In addition to textiles, new industries such as glass, iron, shoes, furniture, and handicrafts came into being. Other nations including Canada, France, Germany, and Japan also had tariffs, but the United States was the ringleader in this respect. This is explored in figure 11.3.

FIGURE 11.3: TARIFFS ON MANUFACTURED IMPORTS IN VARIOUS INDUSTRIAL COUNTRIES (IN %): 1875–1913*

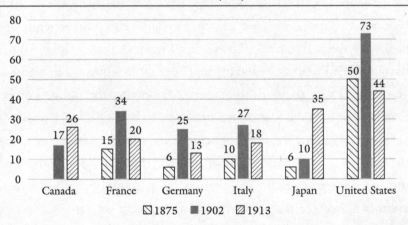

*The Canadian figure is not available for 1875.

Source: The World Bank, World Development Report, Washington, DC, 1991, p. 97; Minami, The Economic Development of Japan, p. 194; Batra, The Myth of Free Trade, p. 178.

By 1902 the average American tariff on manufactured goods had soared to 73 percent, and not surprisingly the nation had already grown into an industrial giant dwarfing all others in Europe. Since production is real income, the United States, in fact, had become the richest nation in the world by the turn of the 20th century.

Why did we then move to free trade when tariffs worked their wonders? There were two reasons—politics and monopoly capitalism. In those days Democrats hated protectionism while Republicans loved it. Following the Civil War, Democratic presidents would try to cut tariffs, while Republicans would ignore them. However, free traders faced a thorny problem, because tariffs were the main source of federal revenue, and trimming them was not feasible without tapping another avenue for taxation. Democrats sought to introduce the income tax, which Republicans abhorred. In politics, the two parties usually have opposing views, regardless of their merits, on economic strategy. Thus, since Republicans championed protectionist policy, Democrats automatically opposed it.

Monopoly capitalism, which was born at the turn of the 20th century, was another reason why the two sides had diametrically opposite views on free trade. Please recall from chapter 4 how robber barons made fortunes by buying up one small business after another and created vast trusts in the process. Following the public outcry, Congress passed the Sherman Antitrust Act in 1890, but it was not enforced for many years. Democrats then felt that free trade was the only way to enhance competition for these conglomerates and thus put an end to their exploitation. So monopoly capitalism was another reason for the rising tide against protectionism.

Until the 1890s few people supported the income tax; Republicans and robber barons decried it as a move toward socialism, but as the shenanigans of monopoly capitalists increasingly came to light, free trade appeared as the only answer to counter their tactics. The media, spearheaded by a newspaper, the *St. Louis Republic*, began to rationalize a low level of income tax. The by-product of this campaign was the Wilson-Gorman Act of 1894, a modest step toward tariff reduction. The act was, of course, challenged in the Supreme Court, which held it unconstitutional.

Democrats then set their sights on altering the Constitution, finally succeeding in 1913, when the 16th Amendment—permitting the income tax—was adopted. The next step was the passage of the Underwood-Simmons Tariff, of which President Woodrow Wilson was the chief architect. This was a monumental change in the tax system and trade policy, but its deleterious effects were not felt until the 1970s, because myriad other events, including two world wars and the Great Depression, overshadowed the response of the US economy. According to economist James Davidson and his colleagues:

> The Underwood-Simmons Tariff of 1913 . . . lowered most rates from 40% to 20% and placed many new items on the free list. *To compensate for lost revenue,* Congress enacted a graduated income tax, permitted under the newly adopted Sixteenth Amendment. It applied solely to corporations and the tiny fraction of Americans who earned more than $4,000 a year. It nonetheless began a *momentous shift* in government revenue from its nineteenth century base—public lands, alcohol taxes and customs duties—to its twentieth century base—personal and corporate incomes [my italics].[4]

Few politicians keep their promises, but one exception was President Wilson, who upheld his pledge of low tax rates—in the first year. Initial income tax rates, introduced in 1914, were minuscule to modest, ranging from 1 percent to a high of 6 percent. However, as tariffs fell further, in order to make up for lost revenue and to finance the needs of World War I, the top-bracket tax rate was raised to 70 percent by 1918 and the lowest one to 6 percent. Falling tariffs thus accompanied soaring income taxes. Those who vehemently argue that free trade helps the consumer by containing prices are obviously unaware of our history. Reducing the tariff indeed lowers the cost of living, but any relief from inflation is more than offset by the income tax that the consumer has to pay in lieu of the import tax. However, even the sales tax decline has the same effect, so there is nothing special about tariff reduction. *Believe it or not, the income tax is the eternal gift of free traders to Americans.*

Every semester, I ask my students if, given a choice, they would rather pay the tariff or the income tax. Ninety-nine percent prefer the tariff, even though most of them have studied the alleged benefits of free trade.

As mentioned above, the momentous switch in tax policy introduced in 1913 was overshadowed by other equally momentous events, such as the wars and the Depression. By 1965, as much as 28 percent of the labor force was employed in American manufacturing, whose wages dwarfed salaries in other areas. (See figure 11.1.) Later, however, as tariffs fell relentlessly in the 1960s and '70s, manufacturing began to erode, and the policy shift started to bite the middle class.

World War II had destroyed the industries of Europe, China, and Japan, while American industry scaled new heights. After hostilities ceased, Western Europe and Japan took about two decades to get back on on their feet. The United States helped both of them to fight the Cold War against communism. By 1965 much of the world had regained its industrial strength while US industry became monopolistic and even complacent against the growing challenge of foreign companies. American labor unions had also grown smug and uncooperative. The quality of foreign goods exceeded that of US goods. Cars produced by General Motors and Ford would begin to break down within two years, even as foreign autos remained sturdy.

As a consequence, after 1965 American exports lagged behind imports. Tariff reduction was the last thing that US industry needed at the time. But monopoly capitalists, whose predecessors had supported protectionism in the 19th century to avert the income tax, now opposed import taxes, and, not surprisingly, so did their hired politicians and economists. Giant corporations, which had already become multinationals, saw free trade as a means of weakening the unions as well as moving some production abroad to take advantage of cheap foreign labor. With tariffs gone, they could bring their low-cost goods back home and sell them at high prices in domestic markets.

Various US administrations successfully pushed trade negotiations around the world, which, slowly but steadily, moved toward globalization. American exports surged, but imports surged more. This was not the sort of exchange that takes place among equals. The hope of someone starting a business is to sell goods in affluent, not poor, neighborhoods, in order to get decent prices. American merchants lost sales to foreign companies but were unable to get the same amount of business from poorer nations.

The United States, which had had a perennial surplus in its balance of trade since 1900, saw the surplus erode in the 1970s and then turn into a deficit in 1981. Even this failed to wake up US economists and politicians. How could it, when the salaries of American CEOs rocketed with growing imports? The trade deficit is a dollar-for-dollar reduction in the demand for domestic goods, and since supply equals demand, the GDP falls exactly by the amount of the trade shortfall. That is why even David Ricardo, the founder of the free-trade doctrine, insisted that all nations benefit from tariff reduction when their trade is in balance.

A simple numerical example further illustrates the point. Suppose American consumers spend $500, of which $100 goes to imported goods. So US merchants lose $100 in sales to foreign merchants. If foreigners buy $40 worth of American products, then the net sales loss is only $60, which equals the trade shortfall. Therefore the fall in the demand for US goods equals the trade deficit, and if demand falls by $60, then the value of domestic output declines by the same amount. So the trade deficit is a dollar-for-dollar reduction in GDP; it causes overproduction and thus layoffs and wage losses.

However, our deficit trade benefited the oligarchs of US multinational corporations, so our politicians remained indifferent to it, even as the American worker paid a heavy price for it. Our foreign transactions have displayed large shortfalls ever since 1981, making the relentless trade deficit perhaps the biggest destroyer of our jobs and wages.

The administrations did whatever the oligarchs demanded from them. On the one hand they permitted wave after wave of business mergers; on the other, they opened up American markets to encroachment from abroad. This was a double whammy, because domestic competition suffered, leading to the production of goods of inferior quality, while low-wage foreign competition intensified. Superior but cheap foreign goods easily vanquished goods made in the United States. Industry after industry disappeared.

First labor-intensive products such as textiles and shoes lost out to foreign producers; then came the surrender from consumer electronics—copiers, typewriters, TVs, VCRs, and cameras, among hundreds of relatively small and light items. Finally came the decline in big-ticket items—tractors, autos, buses, locomotives, appliances, and so on. This was a long process of deindustrialization, which is still continuing. Labor demand and real wages fell in manufacturing, while workers moved into services, so real wages declined in that sector as well. There is no mystery about why the middle class has shrunk badly. The verdict is obvious. *Import restraint built the American middle class, and import proliferation has been slowly killing it.*

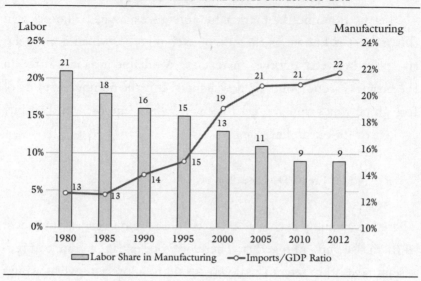

FIGURE 11.4: IMPORTS AS A PERCENTAGE OF GDP AND LABOR EMPLOYMENT SHARE IN MANUFACTURING IN THE UNITED STATES: 1980-2012

Source: Council of Economic Advisers, The Economic Report of the President, *2013.*

Figure 11.4 examines the association between rising imports as a percentage of GDP and the shrinking share of employment in manufacturing. In 1980 the import/GDP ratio was just 13 percent, while 21 percent of workers were employed in manufacturing. Then the import ratio steadily climbed, and the employment share fell to 9 percent, which, you may recall from figure 11.1, is not very different from the 5 percent level recorded in 1800. Back then there was no middle class, which seems to be an endangered species today.

FOREIGN GOVERNMENT INTERVENTION

Why does the trade deficit persist? Normally, when markets are competitive, imbalances automatically vanish in the long run. But our deficit has endured for over three decades since 1981 and still shows no sign of vanishing. So either foreign governments have been intervening in their trade sector or other nations are also dominated by monopoly capitalism. The culprit is in both areas.

Let us examine the market for foreign exchange. The price in this market is known as the rate of exchange, R, which is the relative price between any two currencies. We define it as it is listed in the business section of daily newspapers. It is the number of units of foreign currency you can get for each dollar. Suppose you can buy two euros for one dollar, then

$$R = \text{No. of Euros/Dollar} = 2$$

There are as many exchange rates as there are currencies, but most of them rise and fall together. Therefore, one exchange rate can represent most other rates. The dollar is said to appreciate when it buys more units of foreign currencies. *When a dollar buys three euros rather than two, it appreciates; if it buys one instead, then it depreciates.* Note that the dollar depreciation amounts to a fall in the exchange rate as just defined.

In a fixed-rate system, exchange rates are set by national governments. In a flexible standard, the one that prevails today, they are determined in the market for foreign exchange, as usual, by the forces of demand and supply. In this market the exchange rate is the price, and foreign currency is the commodity bought and sold. The dollar is the principal foreign currency for the rest of the world, so the forces that influence global supply and demand for the dollar determine the foreign price of the greenback.

The world demand for dollars comes from a variety of sources—importers of US goods and services, tourists visiting the United States, and foreign banks and investors ready to buy US bonds and stocks. A trade-deficit nation usually experiences currency depreciation, because the foreign demand for its currency is less than that nation's demand for foreign currency. Take, for instance, the case of commerce between the United States and China, which has a persistent trade surplus with the United States. Since Chinese imports are puny, China's demand for dollars is small relative to US demand for the Chinese currency, the yuan. This should cause a persistent fall in the dollar-exchange rate with respect to the yuan, which would lower the prices of American goods to Chinese consumers and raise the prices of Chinese goods to American consumers, who would then purchase fewer Chinese goods. In a free market, the exchange rate would decline until the Chinese demand for US goods rose to the level of declining American imports from China, leading to balanced trade between the two nations. In other words, in a flexible exchange system, trade deficits automatically vanish in the long run if the foreign-exchange market is free to function.

However, China constantly intervenes in its markets to sustain its export surplus, and does not follow free trade, which requires not only low or absent tariffs but also a free market for foreign exchange. What China does is similar to what speculators do in the oil market; they create artificial demand for oil and thus raise its price. Similarly, China generates artificial demand for the dollar and raises the rate of exchange. America buys goods from China, which in turn buys US goods along with US government bonds. This way the foreign exchange market remains in balance without a dollar depreciation, because

US Imports from China = China's Imports from the US +
China's Purchase of US Government Bonds

As an illustration, suppose the United States imports $100 worth of Chinese goods and China buys $30 worth of American products; then the United States has a trade deficit of $70. The foreign-exchange market now has a large imbalance, which should cause substantial dollar depreciation, raise American exports, and reduce Chinese exports until the market is in balance. But if the central bank of China spends $70 to buy US government bonds, the imbalance vanishes and the dollar remains stable. This way the People's Bank of China has intervened to sustain its export surplus to the United States, which in turn has borrowed $70 from the Chinese government. The US GDP is lower by $70, and the Chinese GDP is higher by that amount. In other words, China keeps its factories humming, while in the United States, they close down. *This way the United States imports goods as well as unemployment from China.*

However, China was not the first nation to adopt this strategy. It was Japan that started this process in the late 1960s and went on an export binge in the increasingly open American markets. By now, though, China has replaced Japan in this regard, and both of them hold vast amounts of Treasury securities. By mid-2014, each nation owned over $1.2 trillion in US government bonds. Many other countries also hold such bonds, but the two Asian nations lead the pack.

Now the question is: Why do these nations want to remain dependent on American markets, when they themselves have large and developed economies? China is the second-largest economy in the world, while Japan is the third largest. Surprisingly, the answer comes from their own growing wage gap.

Recall that the wage gap rises whenever productivity increases faster than the real wage, so that supply rises faster than demand, leading to overproduction and the threat of layoffs. Politicians in the United States postponed this threat by creating consumer and government debt year after year, whereas those in China and Japan simply sent their excess production abroad, because in these nations people like to save money and not borrow much to sustain their lifestyles. See what two Chinese economists, Guonan Ma and Wang Yi, wrote in 2010:

The high saving rate of China has attracted much attention.
The nation saves half of its GDP and its marginal propensity to
save (MPS) approached 60% during the 2000s.[5]

With such a high saving rate, there is not much domestic demand,
so the nation simply exports a large amount of its production. Similarly, China's government debt is tiny, less than a quarter of its GDP.
Japan, of course, has a lower saving rate and a gigantic government
debt, but then its trade surplus is just a fraction of China's. However,
the main point is that if their real wages rose as fast as their productivity, these nations would have no need for an export surplus.

Is there monopoly capitalism in these nations? Yes and no. Japan certainly has made a transition from free markets in the 1950s
and '60s to giant firms since the 1970s, mostly because of business
mergers. The likes of Toyota and Sony abound in the nation, even as
labor unions have grown feeble. As Professor Kang H. Parks wrote
in 2013, "There has been a surge of mergers and acquisitions of business firms over the last twenty years in the world, so too in Japan."[6]
Clearly, industries have become oligopolistic in much of the world,
including Japan, and that is why the wage gap has grown all over
the globe.

However, China is one place where the economy is very different
from that in other nations. The country doesn't have oligopolies, but
according to some it has state monopoly capitalism, in which much of
the industry is owned or operated by the government.[7] While China
no longer relies completely on central planning and has introduced
some market-based reforms, most of its enterprises are funded and
guided by the state. However, regardless of the label describing an
economy, the concept of the wage gap applies to all nations. Whenever productivity outpaces the real wage, there is bound to be overproduction, unless demand is generated artificially, either with new
debt or through exchange-rate manipulation, leading to excessive

reliance on foreign markets. Chinese real wages have grown fast, especially since 2005, but not as fast as labor productivity. Valentina Romei, a journalist for the *Financial Times,* writes:

> The rise in Chinese wages becomes marginal when the increase in labour productivity is taken into account. Chinese labour productivity has been rising sharply at about 10 percent a year since the early 1990s and even more quickly in the past decade, due to technological progress, increased investment and rising human capital.[8]

No matter where we look around the world, the main source of imbalances and economic troubles turns out to be the rising wage gap. This is what we need to restrain in order to rid the globe of poverty and joblessness.

FREE-MARKET OUTCOME IN FOREIGN TRADE

What should the United States do to create a free-market outcome in the foreign exchange market? As stated above, the nations with large export surpluses are not following free trade, and as a result they are slowly killing the US middle class, while our government adopts the attitude of see no evil, hear no evil. Tariffs built the American industrial empire, but they are no longer practical because our economy is globalized and we are a signatory to World Trade Organization (WTO) rules that largely prohibit new tariffs. Apparently, exchange-rate manipulation, as practiced by China and Japan, is acceptable to the world, and so we can do the same. *The point is that we should adopt a policy of balanced free trade*, as preached by David Ricardo, the founder of this doctrine.

There are two ways to achieve balanced trade—export promotion and/or import restriction. In order to stimulate our exports, we can set up an export exchange rate, and to restrain imports, we can adopt some nontariff barriers—which have also been used by other nations—but they should be our last resort.

China does not allow the yuan rate to float freely and, for this reason, regularly intervenes in the foreign exchange market. The nation's objective is to maximize exports. We can do the same. In 2014 the yuan–dollar rate was around six to one; in other words a dollar bought 6 yuan in the foreign exchange market, or 1 yuan was worth 16 cents. This rate certainly was not the free-market rate, or else there would be no trade deficit. While we cannot force the Chinese to desist from intervention, we can do something to obtain the free-market outcome of a depreciated dollar. Suppose our central bank, the Fed, offers a Chinese importer of manufactured goods 25 cents for each yuan. Let's now see what happens to the price of an American good in terms of the Chinese currency. If a pen made in the United States wholesales for $1, and if a dollar equals 6 yuan, then

Pen's cost to the importer = 6 yuan

But if the importer obtains a dollar for 4 yuan, then

Pen's cost to the importer = 4 yuan

The pen's cost in terms of the Chinese currency falls by 33 percent, even though the US wholesale price remains the same. The Fed action would then lower the yuan price of all American products by a third. Chinese merchants would rush to take advantage of the Fed's offer rather than deal with the People's Bank of China and would import a vast variety of manufactured goods into their country. The nation would buy many more cars, airplanes, computers, tractors, cell phones, and so on from the United States. American exports would soar and match our imports from China.

The Fed can make a similar offer to Japanese importers and bring down the price of US goods by a third in terms of the yen. This would balance our trade with Japan. This is all we need to do to sharply lower our trade deficit, because both China and Japan have larger surpluses with us than with other nations, which in any case rarely manipulate currencies to promote their exports. In 2013 China's surplus with us equaled $319 billion, whereas Japan's was a distant second, at $73 billion. Germany and Canada also each had an export surplus with us, but these nations follow free trade, and we need not take any action with respect to them.

China's government should not resist this policy, because Chinese exports to the United States would not be hurt, as a US importer would still buy 6 yuan for a dollar from the People's Bank of China and obtain Chinese goods at the same cost as before. Walmart, Target, and Macy's, to name a few large stores, could still sell the same level of Chinese goods as before. In fact, China should be pleased, because it would no longer be under pressure from US lawmakers to revalue its currency and thus hurt its own exports. In view of the large trade imbalance, it is clear that the current yuan–dollar rate is much higher than that consistent with the free-market equilibrium, according to which supply and demand are equal in a market. The lower rate is required to eliminate the US trade deficit. The Fed action would then create a free-market outcome, even though in reality there still would be no actual free trade, which requires China to abstain from intervention.

If the four-to-one yuan–dollar rate fails to raise our exports to the level of our imports from China, then the Fed should try a three-to-one rate—that is, it should offer $1 for 3 yuan to Chinese importers, because this is one major step toward reviving the fortunes of our vanishing middle class. Suppose the US deficit with China and Japan vanishes; then the US GDP will rise dollar for dollar, that is, by $392 billion, which was our combined deficit with these nations in 2013.

Increase in US GDP = $319 billion + $73 billion = $392 billion

The average manufacturing wage in 2013 was $50,000. If we add another $25,000 for employee benefits and the employer's profit, the cost of hiring a worker becomes $75,000. Then the total number of jobs gained from eliminating this trade deficit is as follows:

New manufacturing jobs = ($392 billion/$75,000) = 5.2
    million

You can see how important it is to trim our trade shortfall, because this action alone would create more than five million jobs. It would rejuvenate our manufacturing, which until 2007 paid higher wages than other sectors. The boost to our economy would be almost immediate, because we already have factories, but they are standing idle, as a large amount of our consumer spending is wasted on foreign goods.

The proposed measure would then generate a two-tier system of exchange rates. One rate, to be fixed by the Fed or the Treasury, would apply to our exports of manufactured goods only to China and Japan, and another would be determined by the global market for dollars. This other rate would apply to all other international transactions, such as foreign investment, imports, and tourism. The Fed—not the Treasury, which has few resources to support this policy—should manage this dual-exchange system. The Fed is an unlimited source of dollars, as has been proved time and again since 2007, and it can buy large amounts of yuan and yen at discounted rates. This way the Federal Reserve will join the crowd of foreign central banks. The Bank of Japan and the People's Bank of China hold vast amounts of dollars or related assets; the Fed would also acquire large levels of yuan- or yen-denominated assets. Just as they buy American assets, the Fed will buy theirs.

BANNING THE EXPORT OF NEW-PRODUCT TECHNOLOGY

Most economists argue that new technology is the main, if not the only, cause of joblessness and low wages in America today. An article entitled "How Technology Is Destroying Jobs" published by *MIT Technology Review* says it all.[9] It sums up the view that has been popular ever since the 1990s, when some people began to question the beneficent effects of free trade for the US economy. This view does not stand up to the testimony of history, because the use of new technology is nothing new. It has been going on for 200 years. It did not hurt us in the past, so why should it hurt now?

There are two types of innovations. One replaces jobs, while the other, known as new-product technology, creates them. In the past those who were laid off found employment in new industries generated by American innovations. Now innovations still occur at American universities such as MIT, but the output resulting from them materializes in low-wage countries. For instance, Apple invents the iPhone, whose production occurs in China, thus depriving Americans of high-tech jobs. In order to fix this anomaly, the government should ban the export of new-product technologies, just as it bans the export of military know-how. We should realize that official policy, not technology, is at fault.

For the sake of national security, we don't allow Lockheed to build fighter jets abroad; restoring national prosperity is also an important consideration, and we should do everything possible to bring it about.

FREE TRADE FOR BIG PHARMA

Another sector that is demolishing the US middle class big-time is known as Big Pharma, which is a nickname for the cabal of giant firms in the pharmaceutical industry. There are 11 of them, spread worldwide, and include such household names as Bayer, Glaxo-SmithKline, and Johnson & Johnson. The stranglehold of monopoly capitalism on the United States is now so strong that there are vast inconsistencies in official economic policy. Economists and politicians alike love free trade, but not when it comes to Big Pharma, which spends more money on lobbying Congress than on research, even though it justifies its outrageous prices for patented drugs by citing R&D spending.

Our patent system awards drug companies a complete monopoly over new medicines for decades, which leaves patients at the mercy of any firm that discovers a new remedy for an old disease. Other wealthy nations are smarter; while they grant exclusive rights to a company with a new drug, they also impose price controls or limit the potential abuse of monopoly power by that firm. A simple way to bring down patented-drug prices dramatically is to introduce free trade in them. Many pharmaceutical companies produce patented medicines in other nations and charge their citizens a fraction of the price charged in the United States. This is price discrimination and is illegal according to antitrust laws. If the Department of Justice were to prosecute the domestic drug companies, they would be forced to lower their prices.

Free trade in medicines will reduce their prices dramatically, although it will increase our trade deficit slightly. This is because the import cost of these medicines is very small. Overall, since the nation spends more than $300 billion per year on medicines, the benefit to consumers dwarfs the cost in terms of the rise in the trade deficit. Balanced free trade is the best policy at this juncture, and the United States should remove nontariff barriers to the import of patented medicines, while taking legal action against Big Pharma for price discrimination.

CHAPTER 12

ELIMINATING GLOBAL POVERTY

THE GREAT RECESSION AFFLICTED THE WHOLE WORLD, INCLUDING NATIONS that were formerly called underdeveloped countries or developing economies. Some of them, such as India, China, and Brazil, have made great strides since 1990; they each now have a sizable middle class. So today it is more appropriate to call them emerging nations.

Some of the emerging markets, such as India and Brazil, are also under the hegemony of monopoly capitalism, which creates exceptional rewards for their oligarchs at the expense of the general public. India, for instance, topped the list of BRIC nations with an expected growth of 17 percent in its millionaire population in 2014.[1] Others, especially those in Africa, Russia, and China, live under the umbrella of state monopoly capitalism, in which factories operate under the guidance of the government and produce high incomes mostly for officials or those with connections to them.

Regardless of the nature of monopoly capitalism, public or private, the sources of poverty are more or less the same. They are the rising wage gap and massive debt creation by the government, so that the fruit of growing labor efficiency goes almost entirely to the rich and powerful. In the preceding chapters I have demonstrated the validity of this conclusion for the United States, Germany, Japan, and China, but it applies to the whole world. Here I will illustrate it chiefly with reference to India and Brazil.

In spite of remarkable strides made by some nations since 1990, a large percentage of humanity around the world subsists in poverty, even destitution. The reason is that our planet's oligarchs, regardless of how rich they are, insist on grabbing their own pound of flesh from any government assistance to the poor. As a result, progress against penury has been excruciatingly slow. A 2014 *Human Development Report* issued by the United Nations reveals that 2.2 billion people, about a quarter of the world's population, live in either poverty or near poverty. South Asia, winning a dubious honor, has the highest concentration of the destitute: almost 71 percent of its people are dirt poor, subsisting on less than $2 a day.

Even more shocking is that just 85 of the world's richest persons own as much wealth as 3.5 billion of the poorest people.[2] Another report by the United Nations focuses on Africa, where poverty has actually grown since 1990. Meanwhile, economic growth around the world has enhanced the global emission of carbon dioxide by 50 percent.[3] That is the real shame of this system, because while billionaires gobble up the lion's share of production gains, leaving crumbs for the masses, the heightened pollution from output expansion is borne by everyone. So the pain is for all, the gain is for the few. Such is the scourge of worldwide monopoly capitalism.

How can you possibly eradicate poverty from the world before the greed of billionaires is brought under control, when there are environmental limits to economic growth? Resources of the earth are finite, while population continues to mushroom. Given the environmental limits on growth, the global economy cannot possibly fulfill the minimum needs of all and end poverty while satisfying the insatiable money hunger of the oligarchs.

We have to devise a system under which labor's efficiency gains are matched by a rise in the real wage. However, at this moment, that is not in the cards anywhere on the planet. So we have to lower our sights and focus on the creation of free-market effects rather than free markets themselves.

INDIA

Among the BRIC nations, India is number one in the percentage gain expected in the number of millionaires in 2014. This is displayed in figure 12.1; Brazil is next, followed by China and Russia. In terms of absolute numbers, though, China wins the race hands down, as depicted in figure 12.2, with India a distant second, and so on. Thus, wherever there is monopoly capitalism, public or private, wealth concentration grows apace. The culprits are the rising wage gaps along with soaring artificial demand resulting from rocketing government debt, consumer credit, and even the trade surplus.

FIGURE 12.1: INDIA TOPS THE LIST OF EXPECTED MILLIONAIRE
GROWTH (IN %) IN BRIC NATIONS, 2014

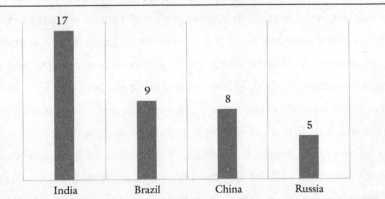

Source: Spear's, *January 2014.*

FIGURE 12.2: CHINA TOPS THE LIST OF MILLIONAIRE EXPLOSION IN BRIC NATIONS, 2014

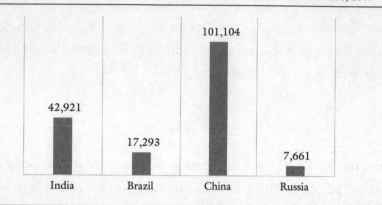

Source: Spear's, *January 2014.*

Relevant statistics are often unavailable for India, but those we have confirm my thesis. One study found that between 1992 and 2001, the real wage in India's manufacturing sector grew 3.5 percent, while productivity rose 5.5 percent, showing that the wage gap went up.[4] Another study discovered something more ominous, similar to developments in the United States. Between 2008 and 2011, India's productivity climbed 7.6 percent, while the real wage actually fell 1 percent. So the wage gap grew even faster.[5]

India used to follow a growth strategy of monopolistic protectionism, which combines monopoly capitalism with high tariff walls—the worst way for a poor country to bring about economic development. As a result the nation suffered rising poverty and unemployment until 1990. However, in 1991 the economy was liberalized; it was opened up to foreign competition, income and corporate taxes fell, and foreign investment and technology were permitted in many more industries. In addition, entrepreneurs were allowed to start businesses without lengthy licensing requirements. As a result of these measures, India's economic performance improved sharply.

FIGURE 12.3: GDP GROWTH IN INDIA (IN %): 2000-2014

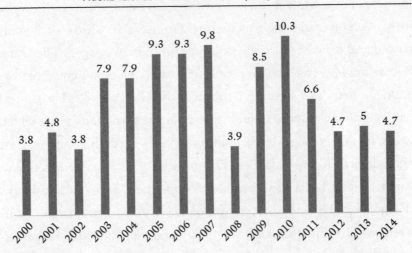

Source: *The World Bank,* World Development Report, *various issues; Planning Commission, Government of India.*

GDP growth jumped, real wages began to rise, and finally poverty began to decline.

India's growth performance from 2000 to 2014 is captured by figure 12.3. From 1950 to 1990, the nation's growth averaged around 3.5 percent per year, but following liberalization the figure jumped dramatically, reaching as high as 10 percent in 2010. However, since then the economy has cooled sharply, and the main culprit is the nation's rising wage gap. The glow of liberalization began to fade, as growth was no higher than 5 percent for three straight years. The chokehold of the rising wage gap is finally overpowering the salutary effects of economic reforms. Another culprit for the slowdown is the high price of oil, which is beyond the nation's control, but if the United States, along with other developed economies such as the European Union, were to act to cool speculation, then the entire world would benefit.

The data we have reveal that the wage gap has been inching up in India. For a while it did not hurt, because consumer credit in the form of credit card loans was soaring. From 2004 to 2007, such loans tripled and delayed the ill effects of the growing wage gap. The Great Recession, however, caught people unaware, and then many borrowers defaulted. The Reserve Bank of India (RBI), like other central banks, sharply reduced interest rates, but the giant banks—of which some, like Citigroup, are US multinationals—actually raised interest rates on credit card balances. This is exactly what has happened in America, and India experienced the same pain. Some Indian banks charge as much as 40 percent annually.[6] So consumer demand suffered, while India's oligarchs made hay under the hot sun. This is exactly the recipe for extreme wealth concentration—rising consumer debt and the wage gap. No wonder India topped the list of expected percentage growth of millionaires among BRICs in 2014.

If the wage gap continues to rise and interest rates stay at lofty levels, GDP is unlikely to grow faster than 5 percent, in which case there will not be much of a dent in poverty, especially in rural areas.

China's growth has also slowed since 2007, but its wealth disparity displays no stagnation. In fact, as mentioned above, the nation was the ringleader in terms of the absolute number of new millionaires expected in 2014. And why not? There, too, credit cards have been proliferating while the wage gap continues to rise. Another reason for China's mushrooming number of millionaires is its trade surplus resulting from exchange-rate manipulation, which creates artificial demand for its output.

BRAZIL

Brazil has followed a dramatically different path in terms of economic performance since 1990. This is another rare case in which a nation's wage gap has been falling since the start of the new millennium, and, not surprisingly, its rate of unemployment has dropped sharply. Available data show that wages have kept pace with labor's efficiency in recent years. From 2007 to 2012, Brazil's productivity index rose by 7 percent, whereas the real wage index climbed by 18 percent, and so the wage gap declined slightly. This was enough to lower the jobless rate from over 12 percent to below 5 percent, which is among the lowest in the world.

However, Brazil's growth performance is as anemic as that of the United States. Except for 2010, growth has been mostly medio-cre, especially from 2011 to 2014, which should be clear from figure 12.4. In 2012 and 2014 GDP grew by only 1 percent per year.

This is mainly because consumer debt rose sharply during the 2000s, as wily banks pushed credit cards into the hands of unwary Brazilians with low initial fees; eventually the people ended up paying insane interest rates, which were as high as 300 percent per year in 2012.[7]

FIGURE 12.4: GDP GROWTH IN BRAZIL (IN %): 2000–2014

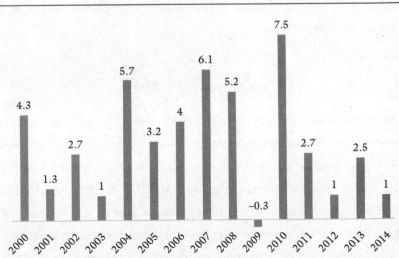

Source: The World Bank, World Development Report, *various issues.*

Why governments allow local and multinational banks to commit fraud and charge confiscatory rates is beyond me. But this is what happened in Brazil for a long time. As a result, Brazil has barely made a dent in its poverty rate even though its wages have marginally outpaced productivity gains.

Historically, wealth concentration has been exorbitant, and that has continued despite the slight decline in the wage gap. Those with large inheritances were able to lend money at enormous interest rates, so the millionaire population continued to climb. In the stock market, banks outperformed other sectors, and why not? Where else in the world can you get away with charging annual interest rates topping 100 percent?

Brazil's poverty rate was higher in 2014 than in 1990. Over 20 percent of its people lived on less than $2 per day. Rural areas fared even worse. The nation seems to have reached a dead end, unaware of what should be done to better the lot of the poor, because exceptionally high interest rates are crippling consumer demand for heavily indebted people. The rate of investment is very low as a result. Clearly, as a first step, credit card interest rates should be lowered sharply through the creation of competitive-capitalism effects in financial markets.

THE PUTTING-OUT SYSTEM

The modern-day factory system is not the only way to produce goods efficiently and provide employment opportunities to all those willing to work at a decent wage commensurate with their education and skills. In fact, it is the least suitable method to alleviate rural poverty, because it requires enormous investment to build offices and factories, where workers assemble to engage in production. It also requires people to migrate to cities, because that is where most large firms are located. As job seekers move out of rural areas, where much of the developing world's population lives, new problems are born in urban centers. That is why in India, Brazil, and China, environmental degradation has surged, traffic jams are common, and urban infrastructure has withered. There are simply too many people in cities, leading to the problems of urban crowding and congestion.

The best way to launch industrialization and uplift village economies in BRIC nations as well as in Africa is a modified version of the old putting-out system, which prevailed in Europe prior to large-scale industrialization. American industrialization following the Tariff Act of 1816 also proceeded along this line. In this system, a merchant middleman, known as a putter-out, supplied raw materials and equipment to workers operating from their homes, later collected the finished or semifinished product, and then marketed it to other users. Semifinished goods were sold to other workers, who then transformed them into finished goods, which the merchant ultimately sold to consumers.

While artisans worked mostly from their homes, usually without supervision, with the advent of power-driven machines, small workshops came into being in cities as well as rural areas. In each, about a dozen artisans would work together under the supervision of a master craftsman. These workshops were precursors of modern factories. As some merchants earned large profits, they expanded their operations, giving rise to large-scale industrialization. For a while, the small workshops and large enterprises existed together, and both were profitable. This shows that small moneymaking firms can coexist with big companies.

The putting-out system worked for centuries and prevailed in all industries, including mining, shipbuilding, paper, pottery, jewelry, iron, armaments, and cotton and woolen textiles, among others. Even today the system prevails in most nations in the form of small businesses; elsewhere, it exists as cottage industries.

India has a large cottage industry that provides a livelihood to millions of people in both big cities and small towns. Ludhiana, the city where I grew up in the 1950s, is a major center of this system. I saw firsthand how men, women, and occasionally their children worked from home and produced yarn, sporting goods, shirts, irons, tables, chairs, and so on, usually without power machinery. The trouble was that they were mostly poor families; I never understood why they lived from hand to mouth. However, now I know the main cause of their poverty. It was not that they produced shoddy products, nor that their costs were very high. It was that the rich middlemen who marketed their products paid them puny prices.

Today also the same problem plagues India's cottage industry. The handloom industry alone provides a livelihood to more than four million people, but they are very poor. However, this setup can be modified in a way to vastly improve their lifestyle.

FROM PUTTING-OUT TO MASS CAPITALISM

In order to create a middle class out of the dirt-poor villagers as well as unemployed urbanites, it is necessary that we use a modified version of the putting-out system. Mainly there are two causes of meager incomes of cottage-industry workers—middlemen and obsolete technology. Old, hand-operated machines generate low productivity, whereas middlemen with high monopoly power offer low prices. Both problems can be solved by the involvement of the government.

First the government should eliminate the middlemen from this business and undertake the task of marketing the products. This step itself would make a big difference, because the middlemen have a markup of at least 200 to 300 percent over what they pay the artisans, whereas the normal retail markup is just 100 percent.[8] So if the artisan's price rises by 50 percent, then instead of living on just $2 a day, the worker would be able to earn $3 a day and rise above the poverty line.

As a simple example, suppose a merchant pays a cottage worker 100 Indian rupees for a product and sells it for 500 rupees. If the government pays the worker 150, uses the normal markup and sells it for 300, then the worker's income will rise and so will the demand for the product, because the price of 300 rupees instead of 500 will attract more customers. Thus, eliminating the merchant's extraordinary profit alone will improve the artisan's lot substantially.

Second, the government should provide new power-driven machines with the latest technology to home workers to raise their productivity sharply. If the village has no electricity, then gasoline-powered machinery should be delivered, and the artisan should be given the option to rent or buy it in installments. With their larger incomes the workers would prefer to buy the equipment, rather than pay rent on it, because in the long run the rental cost is higher than the ownership cost.

Capitalism is a system under which capital goods are owned by individuals or corporations, which in turn produce consumer goods to be sold to the public. When cottage workers begin to buy equipment from the government, then capital ownership will spread to millions of people, giving rise to a new organization of production and a new system, appropriately called mass capitalism. I first wrote about this setup in 2004, but with its implementation through cottage industries, it would move from theory to reality.[9] Mass capitalism is an answer to poverty eradication for the masses, not just in India, but everywhere else.[10]

For a poor country lacking the funds to build expensive factories, this is the most suitable system of production. It can provide a decent living to millions of rural people without displacing them to cities. It is better to utilize scarce resources in obtaining the latest technology than to construct many large buildings to assemble the labor force. Urban unemployment can also be mitigated in the same way. There is no reason why a skilled person is more efficient while working at a factory site than at home. If efficiency rises in group work, then the government can build small workshops in many locations and have people in the neighborhood work there. The products of these workshops can then be transported to a large factory for the final stage of manufacturing, or simply be sold to consumers.

Even individuals and corporations can start such businesses and employ workers living nearby. This would avoid rush hours and traffic jams, because people would not have to travel long to commute to work. But above all, given limited resources, the system would alleviate poverty and keep wealth concentration and the resulting corruption under control. The employees could be paid partly in wages and partly through ownership of company shares.

There is evidence that the new system is starting to catch on. Mr. Apek Mulay, an engineer-cum-economist, has recently authored a book entitled *Mass Capitalism: A Blueprint for Economic Revival*. He argues that mass capitalism is a wave of the future, and I agree.

Let monopoly capitalism pave the way for mass capitalism.

CHAPTER 13

A FREE-MARKET MANIFESTO

WHEN THE ECONOMY SLUMPED IN 2007, FEW EXPERTS BELIEVED IT WOULD turn into the worst recession since the Great Depression. They had great faith in Keynesian economic policies, which rely exclusively on government and consumer borrowing. In an inexplicable irony, administration economists used debt to cure a malady that had stemmed from excessive debt to begin with. By 2014, fully seven years later, a large majority of Americans were unsure about their future, even though the government had spent trillions to restore their battered fortunes. True, the stock market had made a nice comeback, and a few million workers had been called back to work. But after $8 trillion in extra federal debt, employment had barely reached its 2007 level, while poverty was the worst in more than 50 years. In addition, the Federal Reserve had wasted some $4 trillion to bail out the financial system.

Evidently, something has gone awry. Economists and other experts have been confused between cause and effect. They base their policies on what they observe, but what is observed is the effect, not the cause, which occurred many years back. It is this confusion that has led them to cure debt-created ills with heavier doses of debt. Consequently, at most, the status quo has been preserved, but at an enormous cost to the nation and future generations. Something new has to be tried, something that is practical and impervious to the obstructions of our do-nothing Congress. Let us get back to the nitty-gritty of why the nation needed $8 trillion of extra debt, and plenty more from the Federal Reserve, just to restore the status quo, and what needs to be done now to accelerate the recovery. Here is a brief summary of the arguments I have presented.

1. Unemployment occurs if productivity rises faster than wages, because then supply increases faster than demand, leading to overproduction and the threat of layoffs. The threat can be removed through monetary and fiscal policies, which generate debt year after year and artificially raise demand to the level of supply. But this can't be done forever, and when the day of reckoning arrives, it is too late to get out of the slump in a hurry.

2. It is futile to expect banks to increase their lending substantially when consumers are heavily indebted because of several decades of monetary expansion and the resulting puny interest rates. Low interest rates revive demand for homes on one side but lower spending by retirees who depend partly on their savings. Overall, there may not be much benefit from the relentless use of the easy-money policy, but there can be great harm to the economy.

3. Bank bailouts increase speculative activity, because, with people already in heavy debt, Fed-supplied money sits idle in the financial system and finds outlet in asset markets, thereby raising the price of oil and other assets. Low-priced oil helps end the recession, but that avenue has been

blocked this time around so that the recovery remains mediocre.

4. The wealthy support budget deficits and money printing, which not only temporarily stabilize employment but also sharply raise profits and hence CEO incomes. The process gives them more resources to lobby Congress and have laws passed in their favor. So it is not surprising that the rate of profit was the highest ever, or close to it, in 2014.

5. Our persistent trade deficit is among the biggest destroyers of our middle class.

Let us now see what we can do to fix the economy quickly without raising debt and relying on lawmakers.

1. The creation of free markets is the best way to rejuvenate our economy, but that requires splitting the nation's myriad conglomerates into smaller firms, which our Congress will not allow. However, some agencies working for the president can generate free-market outcomes in several crucial industries, which will do the job. For instance, the FDIC can use its authority to legally create what is known as a bridge bank and, through it, offer competition to large banks. This would bring down interest rates on credit card balances from the current average of 15 percent to just 5 percent. Banks are still charging the same high interest rates as in 2007, even though, thanks to the Federal Reserve, their borrowing costs are close to zero. Competition from the bridge bank would sharply lower the monthly payments of credit card holders.

2. Similarly, the Commodity Futures Trading Commission (CFTC) can use its emergency power to raise the margin requirement for buying oil futures from the current 6 percent

to 50 percent, so that the petrol price falls to its free-market level of about \$20 per barrel. In minor recessions in the past, such prices usually fell to less than \$15 and helped speed up the recovery.

3. The Treasury should issue five-year bonds to needy retirees, offering a fixed interest rate of 3.5 percent. This would not raise long-term borrowing costs for the government but would offer a lifeline to pensioners nearly devastated by Federal Reserve policies.

4. The Federal Reserve should intervene in the foreign-exchange market to offer a depreciated dollar rate with respect to the yuan and yen so that our trade deficits with China and Japan vanish. This measure would enable us to follow a policy of balanced free trade and generate more than five million manufacturing jobs within a year.

5. Ideally we should gradually raise our minimum wage and link it to inflation and national productivity, but Congress will not go for it—at least not soon. So the president should continue to ask federal contractors to raise their minimum wage on government-supported work. In competitive markets the real wage rises in proportion to efficiency gains, so that linking the minimum wage to national productivity would simply generate a free-enterprise system in which, over time, the living standard rises for all.

6. In order to preserve competition and avert job losses, the government should not permit mergers among large and profitable firms.

All these measures would raise consumer demand on home goods significantly, enhance the growth rate, eliminate unemployment, increase real wages, alleviate poverty, cut government spending for the jobless, boost tax receipts, quickly eliminate the budget deficit and slowly help retire our debt. Raising the growth rate and real wages are the keys to increasing the living standard for people without luring them further into debt, and these proposals are sure to restore their prosperity.

The free-market manifesto presented above would create competitive-capitalism effects in a number of industries without recourse to Congress. That is why the measures just outlined are practical and can be easily put into practice to bring an end to joblessness, debt, and poverty.

While this manifesto has been developed with respect to the US economy, it applies to much of the world, including developing, emerging, and underdeveloped economies. In addition, poverty-stricken nations should try a modified version of the old putting-out system that preceded large-scale industrialization in Europe and the United States.

There was a time when our government intervened in the economy to generate competition and regularly enforced antitrust laws. However, since 1981, the massive government intervention has taken the form of debt creation at the consumer and the federal level with catastrophic results for the vast majority of Americans. This free-market manifesto also calls for intervention but only to generate competition in various industries. This is the only way to revive the fortunes of the middle class and to stave off hunger, homelessness, and destitution in a nation that not too long ago was the richest in the world.

CHAPTER 14

APPENDIX: A NEW THEORY OF UNEMPLOYMENT

Globalization and the Wage-Productivity Gap

THIS CHAPTER DEALS WITH THE CURRENT STATE OF MACROECONOMICS AND is meant for those who have some familiarity with the subject. The preceding analysis is also about economics, but it is so simple that anyone with common sense can understand it. However, there are some technical issues that require prior knowledge of at least macroeconomics 101, and they are explored here.

Professor Robert Shiller, a Nobel laureate and best-selling author, once remarked, "A great embarrassment for modern macroeconomic theory is that it has never achieved any consensus on the basic questions of what makes the stock market rise or fall and what ultimately causes recessions . . . we have not been able to pinpoint what ultimately causes recessions."[1]

These words are astounding but highly credible. They are astounding because in view of all that has been written about macroeconomics over the past 200 years, you might think that by now we would understand the root cause of unemployment or recessions. They are also credible because a deep slump started all over the world in 2007, and, fully seven years later, its ill effects of high poverty and unemployment continued to afflict the globe.

If we really knew the ultimate cause, unemployment should have vanished soon after the NBER proclaimed the end of the recession in 2010. Instead, in 2012 the official unemployment rate exceeded 8 percent in the United States, and if part-time and discouraged workers are included, it exceeded 16 percent. Even in 2014 employment barely matched the level reached in 2007. The picture was not any brighter around the world. In fact, the eurozone was back in recession in 2011, albeit for a short period, with a jobless rate surpassing 11 percent, which was the highest since its records began, in 1995. In 2014 its jobless rate was even higher.

Professor Paul Krugman, another Nobel laureate, was just as blunt as Mr. Shiller when he wrote, "Few economists saw our current crisis coming, but this predictive failure was the least of the field's problems. More important was the profession's blindness to the very possibility of catastrophic failures in a market economy."[2] Let us face it: The popular theories of macroeconomics, both classical and Keynesian, tell us very little about what ultimately causes a recession or high unemployment, or else the planet would have been free from this scourge soon after the proclaimed end of the slump.

The preceding chapters have already demonstrated that unemployment or recessions occur when there is a persistent rise in the wage-productivity gap. In other words, when labor productivity rises faster than the real wage for some time, a wage-productivity gap develops and ultimately leads to layoffs and a jump in the rate of unemployment. But that is not what popular theories believe. In fact, they contend, sometimes assume, that real wages are proportional to productivity in a market economy, which has clearly not been true for a vast majority of American workers since 1981.

POPULAR THEORIES AND THE GREAT RECESSION

You already know that the American downturn that began in 2007 is now called the Great Recession and was the worst economic crisis since the Great Depression. Millions of workers were laid off, and millions more suffered wage losses and poverty, and continue to do so. The unemployment rate jumped from less than 5 percent in 2006 to 10 percent in 2009. Naturally, a question arises: Did anyone foresee such a calamity? After all, a crisis does not occur in a vacuum. There were all sorts of premonitions of things to come. There was a housing bubble and an oil bubble, along with a torrid stock market between 2003 and 2007.

The general view encouraged by policymakers and academia is that no one foresaw the coming slump. But this is not true. Some of those who base their thinking on empirical models and assumptions, rather than purely theoretical and frequently hypothetical beliefs regarding microeconomic foundations, warned the world in no uncertain terms about the looming crisis. According to economist Dirk Bezemer, "It is not difficult to find predictions of a credit or debt crisis in the months and years leading up to it, and of the grave impact on the economy this would have—not only by pundits and bloggers, but by serious analysts from the world of academia, policy institutes, think tanks and finance."[3] Professor Roubini, Professor Shiller, and I, among a dozen writers, predicted the onset of a recession well before its arrival.[4] In fact, in a book published at the end of 2006 and released on January 9, 2007, I even pinpointed the year in which it could happen. Some of my words in *The New Golden Age* were:[5]

The economy will steadily get worse with home prices falling and layoffs rising. . . .

The housing bubble appears to be a major event, which once had a lot of momentum but is now beginning to recede. Its starting point was 2001, when the interest rate started a panicky fall. It is likely to burst in 2008, give or take a year. The burst could start in 2007 and continue till 2009. . . .

The economy could still face a steep recession because of rising oil prices, but avoid the calamity of a depression. Unemployment could rise to the level of 10 percent or more.

The rest is history. The housing bubble punctured in mid-2007, whereas, according to the NBER, the recession began in December 2007 and ended in July 2009. In addition, the stock markets crashed between October 2007 and March 2009, while unemployment approached 10 percent by November 2010. Thus, some economists did foresee the arrival of the Great Recession, but few macro experts and policymakers paid attention.

Why did most experts fail to heed the advance warnings that were obvious to some? Because, as Professor Shiller remarks, popular theories still "have not been able to pinpoint what ultimately causes recessions." Let us focus on the word "pinpoint," which suggests that there may be only one underlying cause of a downturn. This is precisely what I have argued. Monopoly capitalism, resulting in the rising wage gap and/or oil prices, is the one and only cause of a recession.

While there is only one root cause, there are a lot of symptoms that masquerade as causes in popular macroeconomic models. The classical and neoclassical theorists argue that real-wage rigidity induced by powerful labor unions or minimum-wage legislation results in long-term unemployment. Few policymakers take this idea seriously, although it still resonates with a lot of economists. Furthermore, classical experts contend that the real wage equals labor's marginal product, which is the output of the last worker hired. However, it is the average product, that is, labor productivity, that in relation to the real wage explains what causes recessions and joblessness. The point is that even if the real wage is flexible, as assumed by the classicists, and equals the marginal product of labor—something that fails to occur in oligopolistic markets—layoffs still follow if the real wage does not grow as fast as labor's average product, unless, of course, the economy's debt rises enough to absorb the unsold goods. However, debt growth does not guarantee prosperity for the general public.

On the other end of the spectrum, Keynesian economics suffers from the same flaw, because it also believes that the real wage is determined by labor's marginal product and pays little attention to the role of average product in its theory of unemployment. It is true that there is normally a positive link between the average and marginal product, and their link is exact in terms of a Cobb-Douglas production function. But then we have to assume the existence of a production function, and some economists, especially the legendary Joan Robinson from Britain, have questioned this assumption.

The wage-gap theory does not deal with the issue of what determines the real wage in the labor-market equilibrium; it only focuses on why the wage rate trails productivity growth and how this inevitably causes layoffs in the long run, when debt does not rise sufficiently to raise aggregate demand to the level of aggregate supply. The theory also needs no production function for its validity. Furthermore, even if marginal and average products move closely together, the real wage is less than labor's marginal product under monopoly capitalism.

Keynesians and neo-Keynesians blame recessions on inadequate aggregate demand and see expansionary monetary and fiscal policies as panaceas for the crisis. Such policies were indeed successful for a long time in ending recessions, but, as you have seen, they only postponed the problems. Furthermore, new recessions usually required a stronger dosage of expansionary measures. Now Keynesian remedies either don't work or work very slowly in spite of the massive dosage administered to the ailing patient called the global economy.

They may stabilize the patient's illness but will not, and cannot, restore the patient to robust and self-sustaining health. Moreover, the Keynesian model fails to explain why aggregate demand may remain deficient for a long time, as occurred during the Great Depression and now since 2007. This is a major flaw, because without an understanding of the reason behind demand deficiency, debt creation becomes the only policy option of Keynesian theory. However, the wage-gap thesis developed here offers a variety of options to boost consumer and, hence, investment spending. Debt generation then becomes a minor and temporary way to raise national demand, something to be used only as a last resort.

Another popular theory is offered by the Austrian school, which blames recessions on excessive expansion of money and credit by financial institutions and on the heavy debt burden of consumers prior to the crisis. This view also focuses on the symptoms. The big question is why consumers got hugely indebted prior to the slump. There is no doubt that bank loans and consumer debt rocketed in the United States during the years leading up to the recession. But the question is why! My answer lies in the rising wage gap and ultimately in crony capitalism.

Another major flaw of conventional views is that they are unable to explain the rise of stock market bubbles and their crashes. Robert Hall, a Stanford University professor and president of the American Economic Association in 2010, once said, "Economists are as perplexed as anyone by the behavior of the stock market."[6] He is a macro economist whose popular textbook acknowledges a major defect of traditional ideas. This defect is more serious than may appear. After all, a vast majority of Americans, along with their pension plans, are connected to share values. Furthermore, understanding stock markets is crucial to preserving a nation's prosperity, because their crashes have often preceded debilitating recessions and depressions. The wage-gap theory developed in this book and this appendix is able to provide answers to the questions that perplex economists today.

AN ECONOMIC MODEL

Let us return to the concept of the wage gap, which may be defined as the excess of a nation's labor productivity over its real wage. Suppose this excess is symbolized by β, then

$$\beta = A/w > 1$$

where A is the average product of labor, commonly called productivity, w is the real wage, and β is the wage gap, normally greater than 1, because a part of productivity goes into wages and another part goes into profit. Let Y stand for real GDP or a nation's output and L for the level of employment. Then

$$A = Y/L$$

Normally, the wage-gap index remains constant over time, as the real wage rises in roughly the same proportion as productivity, but in some decades it goes up. When that happens, trouble follows.

In order to clearly demonstrate our results, we begin with one simplifying assumption, namely, that all wage earnings go into consumption, and other types of income from interest, rent, or dividends go into savings. In other words, people do not save anything out of their wages. This assumption will be relaxed later, although it is close to reality for the US economy, in which the general public lives from paycheck to paycheck, has little income from nonlabor sources, and had a rate of saving prior to the recession that approached zero. In fact, in the 2000s the saving rate was even negative in some months. With this assumption, the consumption relationship is expressed by

$$C = wL \qquad\qquad (1)$$

where C is the pretax level of consumer spending. As our starting point, suppose the economy is free from debt and closed to foreign trade. For the time being, assume that government spending and tax receipts are so small that they can be ignored, so that aggregate demand equals the pretax level of consumer and investment spending. Then

$$AD = C + I \qquad\qquad (2)$$

where AD is income-based aggregate demand and I is pretax planned investment. AD thus represents spending by the private sector. Unless specified otherwise, all variables are in real or inflation-adjusted terms. We assume further that investment is proportional to consumer spending. This is a reasonable assumption, because if consumer spending rises, firms tend to expand their operations and add to their investment. So let

$$I = \alpha C \qquad\qquad (3)$$

where α is the response of investment to consumer spending. For the time being, assume that α is constant, so that when consumer spending doubles, investment also doubles. Figures from various issues of the *Economic Report of the President* show that the investment-to-consumption ratio generally varied between 24 percent and 26 percent from 1960 to 2000. In view of equation (3),

$$AD = (1 + \alpha)C \qquad\qquad (4)$$

Let AS be aggregate supply, then

$$AS = Y = (Y/L)L = AL \tag{5}$$

In macroeconomics, Y is commonly used to denote aggregate supply. In equilibrium,

$$AS = AD = Y \tag{6}$$

To all this we add our index of the wage gap expressed by

$$\beta = A/w \tag{7}$$

Thus, our starting point is a simple model with no consumer or government debt and no foreign trade. Layoffs or unemployment in any economy occur when AD < AS and there is overproduction, which is symbolized by X.

$$X = AS - AD = Y - (C + I) = AL - (1 + \alpha)C = AL - (1 + \alpha)wL$$

Or

$$X = wL[\beta - (1 + \alpha)] \tag{8}$$

Note that X is also the value of unsold goods.

In obtaining equation (8) we have made use of all the equations presented above. In equilibrium $X = 0$, so that

$$\beta - (1 + \alpha) = 0 \tag{9}$$

The sophistry of modern economics requires that the rest of the analysis should be presented in terms of calculus, and I do that in an endnote. Here a verbal analysis will suffice. Equation (8) shows that excess supply or overproduction depends on β, the wage gap, and α, the response of investment to changes in consumer spending. If α is constant, then, assuming initial equilibrium, a rise in β, the wage gap, clearly increases X, or overproduction. If α is not constant, then the outcome also depends on how investment responds to the change in β. If β rises, then output grows faster than consumer spending, which means that businesses are unable to sell all of their production. There is no reason for investment to rise, regardless of the value of α; if α is large, then investment declines faster than normal, in which case overproduction also rises faster than normal. In other words, any rise in the wage gap generates overproduction, hence layoffs, unless, of course, consumers go into debt.[7] In this case

$$AD = C + I + CB \qquad (10)$$

where CB is consumer borrowing. We can also introduce the role of the government at this point. Suppose C and I continue to be pretax spending levels by consumers and investors. Let G denote government spending and T denote tax revenue. An injection of G raises AD, whereas taxation lowers it, so that the net effect equals

$$GD = G - T$$

and now

$$AD = C + I + CB + GD \qquad (11)$$

where GD is the government budget deficit. The equation for overproduction now becomes

$$X = AS - AD = wL[\beta - (1 + \alpha)] - CB - GD \qquad (12)$$

For X to be zero in equilibrium,

$$wL[\beta - (1 + \alpha)] = CB + GD \tag{13}$$

Let us analyze this equation carefully. If β rises, the left-hand side of the equation goes up, and if the right-hand side stays constant, then wL must fall, which implies that an increase in the wage gap, with debt remaining unchanged, lowers either employment or the real wage or both. On the other hand, for wL to stay constant, debt must rise. For simplicity let's continue to assume that α is constant.

Equation (13) makes it clear that a rise in β must raise CB and/ or GD for X to remain zero or for labor earnings (wL) to remain unchanged. In other words, an increase in the wage gap generates debt, if the economy is to stay in equilibrium. Since excess supply leads to layoffs, the conclusion is unmistakable: If β rises, then either layoffs occur or debt arises, and in the case of a relentless jump in β, both may occur, as happened in 2008 and 2009. If w were to fall, things get worse, because then unsold goods rise further, so that either layoffs increase or debt has to grow further to maintain equilibrium.

So far we have said nothing about the role of the price level. The model has been so designed that the price level plays only an implicit or secondary role. If goods pile up on their shelves, some firms are likely to lower their prices, but this is unlikely to cure the problem. This is because profits will fall, and some workers will be laid off anyway. Furthermore, falling prices do not guarantee a rise in aggregate spending. Some goods have elastic demand, and some have inelastic demand. So with a general price decline, spending will rise on elastic-demand goods and decline on others. But the economy as a whole cannot have elastic demand, so that, if there is general overproduction, the rise in spending on some goods falls short of the decline in others, as the world experienced so painfully during the

Great Depression. So even if prices fall sufficiently, a rise in the wage gap will generate unemployment, which may even become worse if deflation becomes severe. In any case, there have been many recessions but no price decline since 1960.

AN OPEN ECONOMY

So far we have worked with a closed economy, but it should be clear that opening it to foreign commerce does not change our logic in any way, except that openness may raise a nation's wage gap even further and make matters worse. Let V stand for net imports or trade deficit, which is the excess of imports over exports. Let us suppose net imports are proportional to domestic private spending after taxes, that is,

$$V = \sigma(C + I - T)$$

so that a rise in private spending raises the trade deficit, because a part of the spending increase goes into imports. σ, a positive fraction, may be constant or a function of other variables such as the exchange rate, foreign GDP, and so on. If σ is constant our analysis retains its simplicity and does not change at all, because then

$$AD = C + I + CB + GD - V = (1 + \alpha)(1 - \sigma)wL + CB + GD - \sigma T$$

The equation for overproduction now becomes

$$X = Y - AD = wL[\beta - (1 + \alpha)(1 - \sigma)] - CB - GD + \sigma T$$

And for X to be zero,

$$wL[\beta - (1 + \alpha)(1 - \sigma)] = CB + GD - \sigma T \tag{14}$$

Here again you can see that a rise in β will either cause joblessness or create debt even in an open economy. Since $\sigma < 1$, the overproduction and thus the policy-induced increase in debt are smaller than those in the case of the closed economy. This is because a fall in private spending resulting from a growing wage gap induces a fall in imports and mitigates the decline in AD. If σ is not constant, all that changes is the value of the new debt required to retain full employment equilibrium, because

$$\text{New Debt} = \text{CB} + \text{GD} = Y - (C + I)(1 - \sigma) - \sigma T$$

and a fractional change in σ only changes the value of new debt.

However, there is one significant way in which increased openness affects the outcome. This is because free trade tends to raise a nation's productivity, as demonstrated by Ricardo and many others, and it may also alter the real wage. If a country imports labor-intensive goods and exports capital-intensive products, then a well-known idea of international economics, the Stolper-Samuelson theorem, kicks in and free trade causes a fall in the real wage.[8] With productivity rising and the real wage falling, increased openness itself leads to a rise in the wage gap. Even if national productivity is unchanged, the Stolper-Samuelson theorem shows that free trade tends to raise the wage gap. We may write

$$Y = AL = wL + rK$$

where r is the return to capital and K is the stock of capital. Here national output is divided between labor income and capital income. In the Stolper-Samuelson model, L and K are fully employed and are constant. Dividing both sides of this equation by wL, we get

$$AL/wL = 1 + rK/wL = \beta$$

Since r rises and w falls, free trade raises the wage gap in a capital-abundant nation such as the United States, where imports are generally considered to be labor-intensive relative to exports. The rising wage gap in turn requires an increase in consumer and/or government debt to maintain full employment equilibrium. *All this suggests that a part of the current US debt mountain is attributable to free trade.*

In addition to the Stolper-Samuelson idea, free trade may raise the wage gap if the nation engages in large-scale outsourcing. Outsourcing reduces the use of domestic labor, because a part of home production is done by foreign-based labor. So while L falls, Y remains constant or may even rise, which leads to a rise in productivity. With lowered use of domestic labor, the real wage is likely to fall or at least not rise. Even if the real wage is not negatively affected, the wage gap goes up from increased productivity. *Thus, outsourcing is another reason why the US debt is at its all-time high and is growing apace.*

Free trade may also lower the wage gap, especially if the nation imports capital-intensive goods, where increased openness tends to raise the real wage. Such a nation will then have a very low budget deficit and consumer debt relative to other nations, as is implied by the argument made above. This may partly explain why China, a labor-abundant country, is among the countries with the lowest level of debt.

RELAXING THE ASSUMPTION

So far we have assumed that all wages go into consumption and that savings come from nonlabor income. This assumption is not crucial to our main conclusion that if productivity rises faster than the real wage, then either debt must rise or layoffs will follow. The reason is that *productivity is the main source of supply and wages are the main source of demand, and if the two are not in sync with each other, then the constantly rising productivity along with a trailing real wage creates overproduction, which can be postponed only through Keynesian debt-generating policies.* However, debt is not likely to grow forever, and a point comes when banks stop lending to debt-loaded consumers. That is when a serious slump or a depression follows. In fact, when overproduction occurs, all sources of income fall, and consumer spending may decline faster, in which case the recession is even deeper.

THE WAGE GAP AND PROFITS

We now look at how the wage gap affects the rate of profit. There are two ways to approach this question. Since

$$Y = wL + rK,$$

then dividing both sides by Y yields

$$1 = \pi + 1/\beta$$

where $\pi = rK/Y$ is the share of capital income or profits. Clearly if β goes up, the profit share must rise to maintain the balance in this equation. This is one way to examine this question. Another is to define profit in a macro economy and see what is needed for it to rise in the wake of a growing wage gap.

$$\text{Profits} = Y - wL - \text{Unsold Goods} = AL - wL - \text{Unsold Goods}$$
$$= wL(\beta - 1) - \text{Unsold Goods}$$

As β grows profit must rise if w, L, and Unsold Goods are unchanged. If wL or labor income falls, profits may or may not rise, and may actually decline, because unsold goods then certainly go up. If the government follows a policy of debt creation to absorb unsold goods, then it is clear that profits will rise close to the level of new debt, because then unsold goods fall to zero, unemployment vanishes, and wL may stay constant. All this explains why the rate and share of profits neared their all-time high in 2014.

Yet another way to look at postdebt profits in equilibrium is as follows: Recall that in equilibrium, where unsold goods vanish,

$$\text{Profits} = Y - wL = Y - C,$$

and

$$Y = AD = C + I + CB + GD - V$$

In a closed economy or with balanced trade, $V = 0$, then

$$\text{Profits} = C + I + CB + GD - C = I + CB + GD = I + B \qquad (15)$$

where $B = CB + GD$ is total borrowing by consumers and the government. Equation (15) vividly demonstrates how consumer borrowing and the government deficit enhance the level of profits dollar for dollar. The demonstration requires some special assumptions, such as balanced trade and wages going entirely into consumer spending, but they are not altogether unrealistic. The main point is that the so-called expansionary monetary and fiscal policies that raise borrowing by consumers and the government primarily benefit the rich.

THE WAGE GAP, DEBT, AND THE STOCK MARKET

It seems that experts are still puzzled by stock market behavior, especially amid weak, low growth and in the low-wage economy that has prevailed in the United States since 2010. Professor Shiller voiced his concerns again in August 2014 in an article entitled "The Mystery of Lofty Stock Market Elevations."[9] However, the wage-gap theory, along with monopoly capitalism, easily solves this mystery. Let's assume that share prices (Q) are proportional to profits, that is,

$$Q = \lambda(I + B)$$

where $I + B$ equals equilibrium profits from equation (15), and $\lambda > 0$ represents a link between profits and share prices. Equation (15) shows that, given the level of investment, consumer and government borrowing raises profits by the same amount. As this borrowing has been exceptionally high since 2010, profits and thus share prices have been breaking records, especially in 2013 and 2014.

Profit growth is unusually strong in a low-growth economy, the kind prevalent after 2010, because then the real wage, under the influence of monopoly capitalism, trails the rise in productivity. The rising wage gap in turn ensures a continued rise in borrowing, since the government tries to avert layoffs. Thus it is precisely a weak, low-growth, and low-wage economy that generates what Professor Shiller calls lofty stock market elevations. However, if the economy is exceptionally weak, as in a recession, then for a while no amount of new debt can stabilize employment. At that point profits crash, and so does the stock market.

MAIN CONCLUSION

Our main conclusion is that the rise in the wage-productivity gap because of government policy is the primary, if not the only, cause of recessions, unemployment, mushrooming profits, and, as a result, excessive wealth concentration. These ideas are the same as those

226 END UNEMPLOYMENT NOW

obtained in the preceding chapters, and this appendix adds clarity and reinforces them in terms of what economists call rigorous theory. This chapter also pinpoints the major flaws of conventional thinking, which needs to change if the world is to escape the chokehold of stagnation and poverty.

NOTES

CHAPTER 1

1. For information about the company, see its website: www.calwater.com/about/.
2. Ravi Batra, *Greenspan's Fraud* (New York: Palgrave, 2005); Ravi Batra, *The New Golden Age: The Coming Revolution against Political Corruption and Economic Chaos* (New York: Palgrave, 2007).

CHAPTER 2

1. http://edition.cnn.com/2008/POLITICS/11/04/obama.transcript/, p. 2.
2. http://www.whitehouse.gov/the_press_office/Remarks-of-President-Barack-Obama-Address-to-Joint-Session-of-Congress.
3. http://topics.nytimes.com/top/reference/timestopics/people/w/addison_graves_wilson/index.html.
4. Mitch McConnell in an interview in *National Journal,* October 23, 2010.

CHAPTER 3

1. "Corporate Profits Grow and Wages Slide," *The New York Times,* April 4, 2014.
2. Council of Economic Advisers, *The Economic Report of the President,* Washington, DC, 2013.
3. Press Release, Financial Crisis Inquiry Commission, January 27, 2011.
4. Ravi Batra, *The Great Depression of 1990* (Richardson, TX: Liberty Press, 1985; New York: Simon and Schuster, 1987).

CHAPTER 4

1. CNNMoney.com, http://money.cnn.com/2010/09/20/news/economy/recession_over/, September 20, 2010.
2. A Marist poll reported in July 2013 that 54 percent of those polled believed the nation was still in recession. According to http://blogs.morgan.k12.co.us/jwilson2002/?s=recession, that figure had not changed even in 2014. It concluded, "Although there are people that think that we are no longer in a recession there are people that don't agree and say that we still are in a recession. A new McClatchy-Marist poll shows that 54 percent of respondents think the country is still in a recession and about a third think the recession is over."

3. Lawrence Mishel and Natalie Sabadish, "CEO Pay in 2012 Was Extraordinarily High Relative to Typical Workers and Other High Earners," http://www.epi.org/publication/ceo-pay-2012-extraordinarily-high/, June 26, 2013.

4. Gilbert Fite and Jim Reese, *An Economic History of the United States* (Boston: Houghton Mifflin, 1973), chap. 10.

5. Ravi Batra, *Greenspan's Fraud* (New York: Palgrave, 2005), p. 57; see also Alan Greenspan's chapter in Ayn Rand, ed., *Capitalism: The Unknown Ideal* (New York: The New American Library, 1967), p. 118.

6. "History of Illinois Basin Posted Crude Oil Prices," www.ioga.com; Paul Davidson, "U.S. May Be Inching toward Oil Independence," *USA Today*, February 9, 2014.

7. Elisabeth Rosenthal, "The Soaring Cost of a Simple Breath," *The New York Times*, October 12, 2013.

8. Ravi Batra, "Bailout: The Crisis Profiteering," ravibatra.com, September 29, 2008.

CHAPTER 5

1. Dave Boyer, "That's Rich: Poverty Level under Obama Breaks 50-Year Record," *The Washington Times*, January 7, 2014.

2. Ravi Batra, *Commonsense Macroeconomics* (Richardson, TX: Liberty Press, 2004), chap. 6; see also Batra, "Weapons of Mass Exploitation," Truthout.org, May 8, 2011.

3. Marketwatch.com/thetell/2013/03/28/u-s-corporate-profits-soar-in-2012-workers-get-little-of-it/.

4. Alexandra Stevenson, "Hedge Fund Moguls' Pay Has the 1% Looking Up," *The New York Times*, May 6, 2014.

CHAPTER 6

1. Strictly speaking, output is real GDP, which is not the same thing as national income. But national income is proportional to GDP and is a good approximation for output.

CHAPTER 7

1. John K. Galbraith, *The World Economy since the War* (Boston: Houghton Mifflin, 1994), p. 227.

2. *The Wall Street Journal*, January 2, 2003, p. 1.

CHAPTER 9

1. Takafusa Nakamura, *The Post-War Japanese Economy*, 2nd edition (Tokyo: Tokyo University Press, 1995).

2. Meagan Clark, "ATM and Overdraft Fees Have Never Cost More: Bankrate Survey," ibtimes.com, September 29, 2014.

CHAPTER 10

1. William Engdahl, "More on the Real Reason behind High Oil Prices: Part II," http://www.globalresearch.ca/more-on-the-real-reason-behind-high-oil-prices/9042, p. 2.

2. Council of Economic Advisers, *The Economic Report of the President*, Washington, DC, 2014, 72.

3. US Commodity Futures Trading Corporation, http://www.cftc.gov/about/mis sionresponsibilities/index.htm.

4. David Sheppard, "Obama Oil Margin Plan Could Increase Price Swings," Reuters, April 19, 2012.

5. Bahattin Buyuksahin, "Margin Requirements in Futures Markets," http://buyuk sahin.blogspot.com/2012/05/margin-requirements-in-futures-markets.html.

6. Ray, "Oil Prices Are Dropping Thanks to President Obama," June 29, 2012, http://www.politicususa.com/2012/06/29/oil-prices-dropping-president-obama.html.

CHAPTER 11

1. James Truslow Adams, *The Epic of America* (New York: Little, Brown, and Company), pp. 214–215.

2. Michael Wolff et al., *Where We Stand* (New York: Bantam Books, 1992), p. 10.

3. Courtney Coren, "Poll: Democrats Pessimistic about American Dream," August 8, 2013, http://www.newsmax.com/Politics.

4. James Davidson et al., *The Nation of Nations* (New York: McGraw-Hill, 1990), p. 855.

5. Guonan Ma and Wang Yi, "China's High Saving Rate: Myth and Reality," Working Papers No. 312, June 2010.

6. Kang H. Parks, "Bank Mergers and Competition in Japan," *International Journal of Banking and Finance* 9, February 2013, p. 2.

7. See, for instance, Vahan Janjigian, "Communism Is Dead, but State Capitalism Thrives," forbes.com, March 22, 2010; Gady Epstein, "The Winners and Losers in Chinese Capitalism," forbes.com, August 31, 2010; Adrian Wooldridge, "State Capitalism: The Visible Hand," *The Economist*, January 12, 2012.

8. Valentina Romei, "Chinese Wage Inflation Raises Doubts over Cheap Labour," *Financial Times,* April 5, 2011.

9. David Rotman, "How Technology Is Destroying Jobs," *MIT Technology Review,* June 12, 2003.

CHAPTER 12

1. "The 2014 Millionaire Explosion: Global Stats Revealed," *Spear's,* January 16, 2014.

2. "Quarter of World Population 'Either Near or Living in Poverty'—UN," July 24, 2014, http://rt.com/news/175208-un-development-report-poverty/; *Human Development Report 2014* (New York: United Nations Development Program, 2014).

3. Avneesh Pandey, "Global Poverty Levels Halved but More Africans in Extreme Poverty than in 1990: UN Report," July 8, 2014, http://www.ibtimes.com/global -poverty-levels-halved-more-africans-extreme-poverty-1990-un-report-1621680; *Human Development Report 2014.*

4. Badri Narayan Rath and S. Madheswaran, "Productivity, Wages and Employment in Indian Manufacturing Sector," *Asian Profile* 36 (6), January 2008, pp. 79–97.

5. P. R. Sanjai, Remya Nair, and Anuja Share, "Indian Real Wages Fell in 2008–2011: ILO Report," December 2012, www.Livemint.com.

6. George Mathew and Swarup Chakraborty, "Banks Quietly Hike Credit Card Interest Rates," *Indian Express*, April 4, 2009.

7. "Brazil Interest Rates on Credit Cards Tops 300%, Median Rate in Latin America Is 55%," *Latino Daily News*, July 17, 2012.

8. Merlin Thanga Joy and R. Melba Kani, "Emerging Opportunities and Challenges for Cottage Industries in India," *International Journal of Scientific and Research Publications* 3 (3), March 2013, pp. 1–4.

9. Ravi Batra, *Commonsense Macroeconomics* (Richardson, TX: Liberty Press, 2004 and 2012), chap. 16.

10. Apek Mulay, *Mass Capitalism: A Blueprint for Economic Revival* (Bothell, WA: Book Publishers Network, 2014). This book applies the theory of mass capitalism to America's semiconductor industry and shows how this method of production is an answer for US industries to face foreign competition.

CHAPTER 14

1. Robert Shiller, "The Mystery of Economic Recessions," *The New York Times,* February 14, 2001, p. 17.

2. Paul Krugman, "How Did Economists Get It So Wrong?" *The New York Times,* September 2, 2009, p. 18.

3. Dirk Bezemer, "No One Saw This Coming: Understanding Financial Crisis through Accounting Models," MPRA paper, University of Groningen, Groningen, The Netherlands, 2009, p. 2.

4. Emma Brockes, "Nouriel Roubini, The Economist Who Predicted a Worldwide Recession," *The Guardian,* January 23, 2009; A. Pierce, "The Queen Asks Why No One Saw the Credit Crunch Coming," *The Telegraph,* November 5, 2008.

5. Ravi Batra, *The New Golden Age: The Coming Revolution against Political Corruption and Economic Chaos* (New York: Palgrave Macmillan, 2007), pp. 173, 175, 179.

6. Robert Hall, "Struggling to Understand the Stock Market," *American Economic Review Papers and Proceedings* 91 (2), May 2001, pp. 1–11.

7. Equation (8) in the text says

$$X = wL[\beta - (1 + \alpha)]$$

Total differentials yield

$$dX = wL(d\beta - d\alpha) + [\beta - (1 + \alpha)]d(wL)$$

Since in the initial equilibrium $[\beta - (1 + \alpha)] = 0$,

$$dX = wL(d\beta - d\alpha)$$

Since α responds to changes in β, $d\beta > d\alpha$. Hence a rise in β, so that $d\beta > 0$ or the wage gap rises, makes $dX > 0$ as well. In other words, an increase in the wage gap generates excess supply in the economy and the threat of layoffs.

8. W. F. Stolper and P. A. Samuelson, "Protection and Real Wages," *Review of Economic Studies* 9 (1), 1941, pp. 58–73.

9. Robert Shiller, "The Mystery of Lofty Stock Market Elevations," *The New York Times,* August 16, 2014.

REFERENCES

In addition to the publications mentioned in the notes, I have consulted the following books and articles in my analysis:

Abel, Andrew, and Ben Bernanke, *Macroeconomics* (Reading, MA: Addison-Wesley, 1995), p. 88.

Barro, Robert, *Macroeconomics,* 5th edition (Cambridge, MA: MIT Press, 2000), p. 333.

Batra, Ravi, "Non-Traded Goods, Factor Market Imperfections" and "The Gains from Trade," *American Economic Review* 64, September 1973, pp. 706–13.

——, *The Downfall of Capitalism and Communism* (New York: Macmillan, 1978; Tokyo: Tokuma, 1995).

——, *Surviving the Great Depression of 1990* (New York: Simon and Schuster, 1987).

——, *The Myth of Free Trade* (New York: Macmillan, 1993).

——, *Japan: The Return to Prosperity* (Tokyo: Sogo Horei, 1996).

——, *The Great American Deception* (New York: John Wiley, 1996).

——, *The Crash of the Millennium* (New York: Random House, 1999).

Boskin, Michael, "Tax Policy and Economic Growth," *Journal of Economic Perspectives,* Autumn 1988, 71–97.

Chow, C., and M. Kellman, *Trade—The Engine of Growth* (New York: Oxford University Press, 1993).

Cline, William, *Trade and Income Distribution* (Washington, DC: Institute for International Economics, 1997).

Cooley, Thomas, and Stephen LeRoy, "Identification and Estimation of Money Demand," *American Economic Review,* December 1981, p. 826.

Council of Economic Advisers, *The Economic Report of the President,* various years, Washington, DC.

Feldstein, Martin, "Reducing Poverty, Not Inequality," *The Public Interest,* Fall 1999.

Friedman, Milton, "What Every American Wants," *WSJ.com,* January 19, 2003.

Friedman, Milton, and Anna Schwartz, *A Monetary History of the United States* (Princeton, NJ: Princeton University Press, 1963).

Greider, William, *Who Will Tell the People* (New York: Simon and Schuster, 1992), p. 91.

International Financial Statistics: Yearbook, various issues (Washington, DC: International Monetary Fund).

Kindleberger, Charles, *The World in Depression: 1929–1939* (Oakland: University of California Press, 1986).

Krugman, Paul, "Inequality in America," *Human Rights Monitor,* October 20, 2002.

Lin, T., and C. Tuan, *The Asian NIEs: Success and Challenge* (Hong Kong: Lo Fung Learned Society, 1993).

Marshall, Alfred, *Principles of Economics,* 9th edition (London: Macmillan, 1961), p. 99.

McConnell, Campbell R., Stanley L. Brue, and David A. Macpherson, *Contemporary Labor Economics,* 6th edition (New York: McGraw-Hill Irwin, 2003), p. 229.

Minami, Ryoshin, *The Economic Development of Japan,* 2nd edition (New York: Macmillan, 1994).

Morley, Samuel, *Macroeconomics* (New York: Dryden, 1984), p. 167.

Pierce, P. S., *The Dow Jones Averages: 1885–1990* (New York: McGraw Hill, 1995).

Romer, Paul, "Increasing Returns and Long-Run Growth," *Journal of Political Economy,* October 1986.

Rostovtzeff, M., *A History of the Ancient World* (London: Oxford University Press, 1926).

Saler, T., *All about Global Investing* (New York: John Wiley, 1996).

Sarkar, P. R., *Prout in a Nutshell, 1–20* (Calcutta: Orient Press, 1988).

So, A., and S. Chiu, *East Asia and the World Economy* (Thousand Oaks, CA: Sage Publications, 1995).

Solow, Robert, "A Contribution to the Theory of Economic Growth," *Quarterly Journal of Economics,* February 1956.

Stigler, George, "The Economics of Information," *Journal of Political Economy,* June 1961, pp. 213–235.

Tachi, Ryuichiro, *The Contemporary Japanese Economy* (Tokyo: Tokyo University Press, 1993).

Takatoshi, Ito, *The Japanese Economy* (Cambridge, MA: MIT Press, 1992.

Takuro, Siyama, ed., *Japanese Capitalism since 1945* (Armonk, NY: M. E. Sharpe, 1990).

Toshio, Kurokawa, "Problems of the Japanese Working Class in Historical Perspective," in Tessa Morris-Suzuki and D. Leipziger, *Lessons from East Asia* (Ann Arbor: University of Michigan Press, 1997).

US Department of Commerce, *Historical Statistics of the United States: Colonial Times to 1970* (Washington, DC, 1975).

———, *Historical Statistics of the United States: Colonial Times to 1945* (Washington, DC, 1957).

———, *The Statistical Abstract of the United States* (Washington DC, various years).

Watson, Debra, "Two Decades of Rising Inequality in America," *World Socialist Web Site,* June 8, 2002, p. 1, and November 9, 2001.

Wood, Christopher, *The Bubble Economy* (New York: Atlantic Monthly Press, 1992).

———, *The End of Japan, Inc.* (New York: Simon and Schuster, 1994).

World Development Report (Washington, DC: The World Bank), 1991 and 1997.

Woronoff, John, *The Japanese Economic Crisis* (New York: Macmillan, 1992).

INDEX